Tunnel to
Canto

by
Claribel Alegría
and
Darwin Flakoll

Translated by Darwin Flakoll

CURBSTONE PRESS

FIRST EDITION, 1996
Copyright © 1996 Claribel Alegría and Darwin Flakoll
All Rights Reserved

Printed in the U.S. on acid-free paper by BookCrafters
Cover design: Stone Graphics

Curbstone Press is a 501(c)(3) nonprofit publishing house whose operations are supported in part by private donations and by grants from ADCO Foundation, J. Walton Bissell Foundation, Inc., Witter Bynner Foundation for Poetry, Inc., Connecticut Commission on the Arts, Connecticut Arts Endowment Fund, The Ford Foundation, The Greater Hartford Arts Council, Lannan Foundation, LEF Foundation, Lila Wallace-Reader's Digest Literary Publishers Marketing Development Program, administered by the Council of Literary Magazines and Presses, The Andrew W. Mellon Foundation, National Endowment for the Arts-Literature, National Endowment for the Arts International Projects Initiative and The Plumsock Fund.

Library of Congress Cataloging-in-Publication Data

Alegría, Claribel.
    [Fuga de Canto Grande. English]
    Tunnel to Canto Grande / by Claribel Alegría and Darwin J. Flakoll.
        p.   cm.
    ISBN 1-880684-34-9
    1. Canto Grande (Prison) 2. Prisons—Peru—Canto Grande.
    3. Political prisoners—Peru—Canto Grande. 4. Escapes—Peru—Canto Grande. 5. Movimiento Revolucionario Túpac Amaru.
    I. Flakoll, Darwin J.   II. Title.
    HV9625.C362C36313   1996
    365'.641—dc20   95-37983

published by
CURBSTONE PRESS   321 Jackson Street   Willimantic, CT 06226
e-mail: curbston@connix.com   WWW: www.connix.com/~curbston/

Tunnel to Canto Grande

INTRODUCTORY NOTE

On July 9, 1990, forty-eight political prisoners escaped from the infamous Canto Grande, the maximum security prison just outside Lima, Peru, executing a daring plan that took three years to carry out in coordination with their compatriots on the outside. A few weeks later, Claribel Alegría and Darwin J. Flakoll accepted an invitation from a guerrilla group to interview the escapees and their collaborators in a safe-house in Peru and to fashion a narrative about their escape from the "escape proof" penitentiary. The participants, Members of the Peruvian Tupac Amaru Revolutionary Movement, described their construction of the tunnel, the human conflicts and passions involved, including fear of betrayal by one member and the romance that developed between two others, the disappointments, and their final successful escape, where the only "casualty" was one guard bopped on the head with a soda bottle. *Tunnel to Canto Grande* is their story.

CHAPTER 1

Life, Jaime reflected as he paused to pass a hand across his sweaty brow, is just one damn tunnel after another. He was seven meters underground; the air at the tunnel face was dead and thick with the stink of his own perspiration, and it was hot, hot, hot! The only illumination was a dim bulb hanging from a spike in the wall just behind his shoulder. He groped backward along the floor until his hand connected with the water bottle. He unscrewed the cap and took several deep swallows before recapping it and setting it down. All four diggers consumed gallons of water each day during their work shifts and promptly converted it into perspiration that streamed down their naked chests and mixed with the grainy sand filtering from overhead to become a slick mud that clung to their bodies.

At the moment, Jaime was confronting his daily adversary: an inanimate enemy in the form of a large boulder that protruded from the face of the tunnel. It was another of the hundreds that slowed their advance to a painful twenty centimeters per day. He sighed, fitted the pointed wedge of hardwood beneath the large rock and tapped its cloth-padded butt end with the sledge hammer. He moved the wedge, tapped again, and freed a chunk of compacted sandy soil that fell to the floor at his knees.

The tunnel was painfully constricted: a mere eighty centimeters high by sixty wide. Jaime was forced to work on his knees or squatting on his haunches until his leg muscles trembled. He was kneeling at the end of a tunnel that reached from the operational base in the safehouse, beneath the street fronting it, and was now inching forward under the row of fenced-in vacant lots across the street. His tools were limited to the padded wooden wedge and hammer because sound carries underground, and the diggers couldn't risk the chance that some casual passerby might detect the clang of metal on metal reverberating through the earth. Even worse, the sounds of excavation might arouse the suspicions of the *Republicano* prison guards who occasionally patrolled the area, making security checks.

The most frustrating thing about his present grueling occupation was that the team wasn't tunneling toward their objective but away from it. The lengthy detour was necessary because the area behind the safe house was occupied by a commercial sandpit that grew deeper week by week as a clamshell digger loaded heavy dump trucks that trundled in and out of the pit. That obstacle standing between their operational base and Canto Grande made for excellent cover, of course. Who would ever suspect that the modest, walled-in house on the far side of the sandpit might be the site of a tunneling operation designed to penetrate beneath the high brick walls of the state penitentiary itself?

Jaime sneezed, nearly blowing off the surgical mask that covered his face and mouth. The mask made it even more difficult to suck the dead air in and out of his lungs, but it was necessary to prevent him from inhaling the sandy dust from the digging. The sneeze, he feared, marked the onset of another cold, the common occupational hazard of all the diggers. The temperature at the tunnel face frequently reached forty degrees centigrade, and the contrasting temperature of the air at the surface when they ended their day's work might be as much as fifteen to twenty degrees colder. Colds and bronchial infections were the most frequent ailments assailing the team, closely followed by headaches brought on by the lack of oxygen, and intestinal complaints resulting from their unhygienic work environment. Despite Paloma's competent ministrations and concern for their diet, one or another of them was always under the weather and only held to the daily work schedule by sheer force of will.

Grim as Jaime's present working conditions were, they were idyllic compared to those of his first tunnel. His nose wrinkled in disgust as he recalled wading through the shit and slime of the sewage duct beneath Canto Grande to reach the excavation site, remembered the three weeks he and the others spent chipping a hole through the concrete wall of the duct before they could even start the excavation itself. And then the only way to get rid of the dirt was to remove it, sack by sack, and scatter it evenly along the bottom of the sewage channel, hoping that the prison guards would not notice the gradually rising sedimentary layer in the duct.

Getting rid of the dirt had been the chief problem in excavating that first tunnel inside the prison walls, just as it was becoming the principal obstacle in this dig. The battered old taxi that was the safehouse's only operational vehicle could haul away no more than six to eight sacks of dirt on each of its two daily trips, and it was increasingly subject to breakdowns.

What they needed, he realized, was a large pickup truck with a canvas-covered frame over the truck bed to conceal the sacks of dirt it would be carrying. Light cargo haulage was a common marginal occupation in Lima, and a pickup truck would be less conspicuous than the ancient taxi traveling back and forth in this lightly populated area of the city. He nodded to himself in the semidarkness. He would bring up the idea after dinner tonight when they held their daily evaluation session.

At the moment, however, the boulder demanded his attention. He had freed the dirt around it on all sides and now he laid down the hammer and put all his strength into breaking it loose. Using the wedge as a lever, he tried joggling it left and right, then up and down, and he thought he felt it move a fraction of an inch. He was an obstetrician in a surgical mask engaged in the forceps delivery of a forty-kilo fetus from Mother Earth's womb.

Jaime is a well-muscled young man of medium height—clandestine tunnel diggers should not be overly bulky or tall—and he speaks rapidly, striking the air with decisive gestures as he tells his story. We are sitting in the dimly illuminated bedroom of a safe house in an unidentifiable district somewhere in Lima, Peru. The single window in the bedroom and the smaller one in the bathroom are covered with black polyethylene taped to the frames. Downstairs, a radio plays rock music, *criollo* waltzes, Golden Oldies from the 40s and 50s all day long and well into the night. Jaime sits on a chair facing us, speaking into the tape recorder that lies atop the double bed. He speaks in a low voice that has become second nature over the years. Inhabitants of safe houses must remain invisible and must not raise their voices. We occasionally prompt him to speak louder so the tape recorder will register his words.

Jaime is the son of a provincial schoolteacher who was a member of Victor Raúl Haya de la Torres' APRA party. Economic circumstances prevented him from continuing his studies beyond the secondary level. Instead, he moved to Lima and worked as a factory hand in the industrial belt ringing the city. Later, he became a civil construction worker — a bricklayer — and by 1983 he was an active mid-level leader in the Peruvian Construction Workers' Union. His years of participation in the lower reaches of the Peruvian working class honed the radical ideology he had inherited from his father and inflamed his indignation at the obvious and inherent injustices of Peruvian society. Jaime is determined to do his utmost to change that society.

The only Peruvian revolutionary movement engaged in armed struggle in the early 80s was the Maoist *Sendero*

Luminoso (Shining Path) whose senseless violence and dogmatic fanaticism were repellent to Jaime's ampler view of the world. But by early 1984 he began reading about the exploits of the newly organized *Movimiento Revolucionario Tupac Amaru* (MRTA), an urban guerrilla group that operated principally in the nation's capital.

"I was attracted to the MRTA," he tells us, "because its leaders always set an example for the rest. They were out in the forefront of every operation, risking their own skin."

Working-class friends who had watched his union activities invited him to join the new revolutionary organization, and Jaime accepted. In a short time he was risking his skin along with the rest of his new comrades.

After a year's militancy, Jaime was arrested in April 1985, while taking part in an "economic recuperation" (read bank stickup). He was routinely interrogated, tortured, and sentenced to two years in the new maximum-security detention center on the outskirts of Lima—the Miguel Castro y Castro penitentiary, commonly known as "Canto Grande" — when it opened in early 1986.

There he joined the growing number of MRTA militants who had fallen prisoner, most of them in circumstances similar to his own. These "politicals" had established their own territory on the fourth floor of Pavilion 2-A inside the prison, separating themselves from the common prisoners, the drug traffickers, and from the "*Senderistas*" who had jealously isolated themselves from all contact with the other inhabitants of Canto Grande.

It had been a rough two years, Jaime acknowledged, and the worst part came at the very end of his term, from May to July 1987, when he had volunteered to take part in the digging of a tunnel from the sewage duct that ran beneath each of the prison pavilions toward the closest section of the outer wall.

That first escape effort was aborted when prison guards discovered the twenty-meter tunnel on July 16, 1987. The authorities were unable to determine which group of prisoners was responsible for the dig, and since the MRTA group was confined on the fourth floor of their pavilion, suspicion did not fall heavily on them.

On July 23, 1987, exactly a week after the tunnel was discovered, Jaime was handed his release papers and suddenly found himself a free man. He immediately set about establishing contact with his organization.

"I made contact with the *compas* over the weekend, and I was told to lie low for a few days. Then, four days after my release, I was visited by somebody from the Directorate, and guess what he told me." He leans back in the chair, spreads his arms and grins ruefully. "He said that my next assignment was to dig a tunnel from the outside back into Canto Grande." He shakes his head at the memory.

Here he was, wrestling the boulder free and easing it to the floor. He dragged it back along the tunnel a few feet to where his shift partner could get at it and haul it to the tunnel entrance. He stepped over it, returned to the tunnel face and wearily picked up his hammer and wooden wedge.

"Hi-ho, hi-ho," he hummed, "it's back to work we go..."

He was one of Snow White's dwarfs, delving in search of subterranean gems. Paloma was Snow White, naturally, and he himself was Grumpy or — his nose itched intolerably and another internal explosion shook him — no, he could be no other than Sneezy. The best part of the day came when his shift ended, he showered in the underground cubicle and changed into clean jeans. Then, relaxing with his arms folded over the back of a kitchen chair, he would submit gratefully to Paloma's gentle hands, cleaning the cuts and abrasions that all of them inevitably accumulated each day. She would paint them with merthiolate and then knead Sloan's liniment into his aching back and shoulder muscles: a fifteen-minute massage such as only saints and angels in Paradise enjoy.

Stop it, he admonished himself. Paloma had also explained that the lack of oxygen and the increased carbon dioxide in the tunnel made one susceptible to psychedelic visions and hallucinations. And who needed that?

The next best hour of the day came after the massage, when he stretched out on the living room floor with a good book. He was reading Omar Cabeza's epic of the guerrilla struggle in northern Nicaragua now, and he envied the latter's vagabond existence, wandering through the green jungles of the Segovias with parrots and monkeys for company. Just as he envied the life of his own guerrilla comrades of the MRTA who were camping in the Peruvian jungles on the far side of the *cordillera*. Absolute freedom, he thought, and a total contrast to his own cramped, confined, underground toil. He recalled Sandino's letter to a friend in which he prophesied that, after he died and was buried, the ants would excavate tunnels to his tomb and inform him as to how the national liberation struggle was progressing.

I'm one of Sandino's ants, he thought, as he paused to uncap the water bottle again, and it's the same struggle the world over. He swallowed thirstily and recapped the bottle. Or no, his thought continued, I'm just another Peruvian *cholo* who, like a damn fool, volunteered for the *mita*, and here I am, tunneling back through two hundred years of time to inform old man Tupac Amaru himself that we're still carrying on with the job he bequeathed us.

THE TIME TUNNEL-I

For the Peruvian Indian under the Spanish Empire, nothing was more odious or humiliating than his forced labor in the *mita:* an obligatory period of ten months which he spent tunneling into the fabulous treasure trove of the Potosí silver mines. He had to leave his native village, pay his own travel expenses to the High Andes in what is now the southern part of Bolivia, and there, under the lash of cruel overseers, take on the thankless, inhuman task of opening interminable tunnels in the earth, 5000 meters above sea level.

The Count of Alba, a Peruvian viceroy of the seventeenth century, wrote that "...the stones and minerals of Potosí are bathed with Indian blood, and if one were to squeeze the money extracted from them, he would wring out more blood than silver."

The pitiless Visitor General who drowned in blood the insurrection led by Tupac Amaru in 1780—José Antonio de Areche—wrote in private correspondence some three years earlier that "no heart is strong enough to withstand the spectacle of Indians being driven from their homes into forced labor forever, because out of a hundred who leave, scarce twenty return."

CHAPTER 2

Margarita arose well before dawn, because today —
Saturday — was visitors' day. Since she had no refrigerator,
she had already parboiled the chicken the night before, and
now, when the charcoal was glowing under the grating, she
placed the pot over it, sliced onions, carrots, and potatoes
into the rich broth, and added a few pinches of salt. It was
daylight by the time she sipped a spoonful, decided it was
ready, and removed it from the fire. She made a nest for the
pot in the bottom of her shopping bag, which contained a
pair of worn tennis shoes, patched but clean denim pants,
an undershirt, and a handkerchief. She screwed the pot lid
down tightly over the food and left the small house, locking
the door behind her. The solidarity collection had been
better than average the day before, and on the way to the bus
stop she stopped in at the neighborhood bakery to buy two
loaves of bread and at the corner grocery to buy a dozen
bananas and three packs of cheap cigarettes. Her boys would
have a fine meal today.

She had to transfer twice before boarding the aged bus
that would take her to her destination, hunching her
shoulders for endless minutes at each bus stop to ward off
the chill of the dank gray morning. She placed the shopping
bag at her feet as the bus turned eastward and crossed the
dry riverbed to trundle through increasingly impoverished
neighborhoods of sketchy houses and dusty streets toward
the barren foothills of the Andes.

All the houses in the slum areas ringing metropolitan Lima appear unfinished, although all are inhabited. Many of them have only one usable room, occupied by the resident family, while the rest of the structure must wait until the owner can afford to add a bathroom or kitchen, or even a living-dining room. Invariably, concrete columns with steel reinforcing bars sprouting from their tops project a few feet above the flat roofs of each house in mute testimony to the Peruvian householder's invincible optimism that someday, somehow, he will be able to add a second story to his home.

The bleak octagonal fortress of the "Miguel Castro Castro" maximum security penitentiary is set back into the very edge of the alluvial plain that fringes the bleak grayish-brown hills marking the beginning of the *cordillera*. Huge boulders cover the slopes behind the prison, but there is not a single tree nor a touch of green to relieve the stark landscape.

Though it was not yet 8 a.m., the visitors' queue, composed entirely of women, had already started forming when Margarita arrived at the three-meter-high concrete-block wall some hundred meters distant from the outer wall of the prison itself. She took her place at the end of the line, chatting desultorily with the mothers and wives of other inmates as she waited for the visiting hours to begin.

The recently inaugurated, full day visits from 9 a.m. to 5 p.m. represented a triumph for Margarita and others like her, who had spent the past years waging a patient war of public protest against the corruption of prison officials and the inhuman conditions in which the prisoners were forced to live. Her own son, Roberto, had been one of the first political prisoners remanded to the brand-new, escape-proof prison commonly known as "Canto Grande" when it opened in early 1986. She shook her head ruefully as she recalled the security system that had been enforced in those early days. She had had to go through the lengthy bureaucratic process of obtaining her electoral identification card with her photograph, fingerprint, and signature before she was permitted to visit her son for ten minutes every other Wednesday. The so-called "visits" took place in a room containing a double row of booths divided by a thick glass wall. She sat at a desk equipped with a telephone and talked to Roberto, who sat on the other side of the glass wall facing her, listening over another telephone, and the conversations were automatically taped. When the telephones stopped working, as they soon did, small grilled openings were cut in the bottom of the glass, and one had to bend down and put an ear to the opening while the other shouted a message and then bent down in turn to listen to the reply. Policemen roved the corridors behind the line of booths to make sure no written messages were passed between visitors and inmates.

She sighed gratefully. The new system was blissful compared to what had gone before, but it hadn't been a free gift by any means. The mothers and wives, and the prisoners themselves, had been forced to fight every inch of the way to achieve the new relaxation of the rules.

At 9 o'clock, a prison guard appeared at the head of the queue and seated himself at an open-air desk against the wall. Each visitor in turn stopped before the desk to receive a numbered tag. The guard wrote the tag number in indelible ink on the visitor's upper forearm, then added the number of the prison pavilion the individual wanted to visit, and finally placed the indelible prison stamp near the wrist. When Margarita had completed this procedure, she picked up her shopping bag and passed through the first entrance gate, to walk up a sloping ramp toward the prison proper with its high brick wall and guard towers at each of the eight salients.

The guard tower closest to the prison entrance was Tower No. 8. Margarita knew that the Guards were authorized to fire at anyone making suspicious movements in the no-man's-land outside the wall or the other cleared,

20-meter strip inside it. Before reaching the Admissions entrance, she turned aside and took her place in another queue before a shed with thatched roof where she was given a form to fill out. This, Margarita accomplished with some difficulty inasmuch as her native tongue was Quechua and her imprisoned son, Roberto, had taught her to read and write only a year or so before his arrest.

First, she listed the number on her tag and forearm, her name and home address, and the serial number of her identity card. On the bottom half of the form she wrote the pavilion number and the name of the prisoner she intended to visit. Two guards at the exit end of the shed picked up her numbered tag, compared it with the number on her forearm, inspected the form she had filled out, and checked the information against that on her identity card. While one of them collected the tag, the form, and her identity card, the other wrote the number of the pavilion on her other forearm and stamped her with the penitentiary seal.

She had to endure still another queue at the admissions entrance to the prison. A male guard emptied the contents of her shopping bag onto a table and inspected them, while a female guard escorted her into a small cubicle and performed a body search. Margarita particularly detested this part of the entrance procedure, because roughly half of the police matrons assigned to this detail were lesbians who pawed their victims obscenely and suggestively.

Margarita returned to the outer office and began to reload her shopping bag. The guard nudged the packs of cigarettes.

"There's a limit of two packs, you know."

Margarita knew he was lying, and the guard knew she knew he was lying. She picked up the third pack and handed it to him resignedly.

"Then why don't you keep this one?" she said.

"*Chévere,*" he agreed cheerfully and waved her on through with her bulging shopping bag.

Nearly all the other women in line were also carrying shopping bags and packages, each of which had to be inspected for forbidden materials. No fermentable fruits such as oranges and pineapples were permitted inside the prison, Margarita knew, because the prisoners invariably used them to make *chicha*, a fermented fruit drink that provokes splitting headaches. Relatives of prisoners, however, were encouraged to bring food supplies in for the inmates, because the absurdly low per-capita food allowance was systematically skimmed by corrupt prison administrators, and the daily fare served up to the prisoners was watery slop.

The ordeal of admission to the prison itself had ended, and Margarita trudged through the narrow tunnel of the single entrance to the prison proper and entered the concrete circle running around the central rotunda where prison guards were on duty twenty-four hours a day in the glassed-in second story that offered them an unobstructed view of the inner compound with its six four-story pavilions arranged like the spokes of a wheel around the central hub. One last guard inspected the pavilion number on her forearm and waved her toward the entrance of Pavilion 2-A where the MRTA political prisoners were housed on the fourth floor.

The receptionist at the chain-link gate on that particular Saturday happened to be Ciro, who squeezed her hand warmly as he ushered her inside and asked:

"What did you bring us today, Auntie Margo?"

"A delicious chicken stew." She patted the shopping bag.

"You'll find Roberto in the library," Ciro told her. "Go right on up."

Ciro comes from an Andean province. In 1983, when studying medicine at San Marcos University in Lima, he made contact with the MRTA. The *Sendero Luminoso* had been active for several years at that time, but he considered it "a terribly sectarian organization, much too authoritarian and dogmatic to suit me."

He joined the MRTA and during the next two years took part in a number of "armed propaganda" operations. The MRTA was undergoing growing pains during that period and accepted new members without paying sufficient attention to security precautions. A police infiltrator penetrated their ranks, and in October 1985 a number of MRTA members and sympathizers were rounded up, and some of them were killed. Ciro was among those arrested, and though there was no specific evidence of wrongdoing against him, he was sentenced to a year in the Lurigancho prison.

After his release, he spent another year working for the organization, until the end of 1986 when he was caught entering a safe house that had been spotted and staked out by the police. He was carrying false identity papers in the name of a youth who had died, and when this name appeared in the press, the father of the dead boy presented himself to the police and protested that Ciro was not his son. Ciro was tortured in an effort to get him to reveal his true identity, but he refused to talk. At that point, however, members of his own family came forward and revealed his true name in the course of presenting a writ of *habeas corpus* to free him from the clutches of DIRCOTE (*Directorio Contra el Terrorismo*), the savage Peruvian Directorate Against Terrorism that systematically tortures political prisoners while interrogating them, before turning them over to the judicial authorities for trial and sentencing. This time, Ciro was sentenced to Canto Grande, where he was to spend the next three and a half years.

When he arrived at Canto Grande, the thirteen prisoners of the MRTA were housed in Pavilion 3-A on the second floor, with common prisoners occupying the third and fourth floors above them. This situation proved intolerable.

As Ciro explained, "to live alongside the poorest prisoners means you are constantly exposed to petty thievery. And those people are also the worst troublemakers. After we evaluated the situation, we mounted an operation to move to the fourth floor of Pavilion 2-A, which was much more tranquil."

This decisive move occurred after a violent confrontation with the ringleaders and strong-arm squads among the common prisoners in Pavilion 3-A and was made possible because the *Republicano* police force had just been assigned responsibility for internal security in the penitentiary and didn't yet understand how the system functioned.

The "Miguel Castro Castro" maximum security penitentiary was inaugurated in early 1986 with a fanfare of publicity touting it as Peru's first escape-proof prison where only the most dangerous delinquents would be incarcerated. Prisoners were to be confined in their cells day and night, cell blocks would be locked at all times, and closed-circuit television cameras would constantly scan each floor of every pavilion so that guards on duty in the central rotunda could monitor every portion of the prison twenty-four hours a day. Even beneath the foundations of the prison itself, according to the press, electronic sensors were planted deep in the soil at regular intervals to detect digging noises that would betray the location of any possible escape tunnel. The octagonal design was sound, with its eight guard towers in the outer wall, each with a powerful spotlight and lens of bulletproof glass, and unobstructed free-fire zones in all directions. The system gave every appearance of being escape proof.

At the end of 1986, when Ciro arrived, Canto Grande was run under strict "lock-up" rules. Prisoners were locked in, two to a cell, twenty-four hours a day, except for a five or ten-minute period when they were allowed to stretch their legs in the pavilion patio. Visits by family members were limited to once every two weeks, under strict surveillance; contact between prisoners and visitors was forbidden; and no children were allowed inside the prison.

The decade of the 80s was marked by a vertiginous spiral of criminal activity, drug trafficking, and political violence. The Peruvian judicial system became clogged with a backlog of pending trials, and the national prison system bulged and threatened to burst at the seams. By 1984, as an example, the Chorillos prison, designed for 250 prisoners, was forced to accommodate 700, while Lurigancho, with a planned capacity of 2400, held 5500. Other prisons, such as *"El Frontón"* and the Santa Barbara women's prison, were equally overcrowded. It was because of this inexorable explosion of the prison population that Canto Grande was built to house those considered to be the most dangerous offenders.

Canto Grande was designed to hold a maximum of 700 prisoners, each in solitary confinement in his own cell and under constant surveillance by the turnkeys in the cell block. A year after it opened, however, there were two inmates assigned to each cell, and the number kept growing until there were three, and eventually four. Concrete slabs were installed as double bunks, severely limiting the space in each cubicle.

The Peruvian government, to preserve a maximum-security system of incarceration, would have had to build at least the equivalent of one new Canto Grande each year, but the economic crisis of the 80s hit Peru harder than most other Latin American nations, and there were no public funds available for such niceties as comfortable prisons. Faced with this overcrowding, prison officials inevitably had to relax the strict security measures that had been enforced at the beginning.

The influx of visitors had slacked off, and Ciro found himself alone at the entrance gate to Pavilion 2-A. The guard facing him in the rotunda fishbowl was poring over a sheaf of papers — probably the forms turned in by the morning visitors — and Ciro casually leaned back against the barred gate and rested a hand on the heavy slab of the built-in lock. He had spent the past few minutes surreptitiously rolling filaments of copper wire from an electrical cord into a loose ball, and this he now inserted in the keyhole of the lock. He tamped it deeper into the lock with a wooden matchstick, until it was invisible from the outside. He yawned, stretched and smiled beatifically up at the rotunda guard who had just looked up from his paperwork to glance around his sector of the compound and make sure everything was tranquil.

Margarita stolidly climbed the four flights to the MRTA aerie. At the head of the stairway, she turned left onto the pavilion balcony overlooking the central compound. This space was set aside as the kitchen for the cellblock and was equipped with a charcoal stove: no combustibles, such as kerosene or gasoline, were allowed inside the prison. Roughly half the floor space was covered with bottles, cans, and miscellaneous containers filled with water. Canto Grande's water supply only functioned from 9 to 9:30 each morning, and prisoners had to line up for showers and fill all available containers with water for drinking and cooking during that short interval, or else go without.

She greeted Ernesto, who was serving on the cooking detail that day, and extracted the bread, the bananas, and the pot of chicken stew from her shopping bag. Ernesto tugged off the tight cover of the pot and sniffed appreciatively.

"All it needs is reheating at noon," she assured him, "unless you have some vegetables to add to it."

He shook his head, grinning.

"Quique's mother brought us a big bowl of pasta with cheese, so we're going to have a real banquet," he enthused. "Don't you worry about a thing."

Margarita picked up her shopping bag again and walked through the open cellblock door into the corridor, lined with barred windows on the right-hand side and with eight cells on the left. All the cell doors were open, and, inside, a few inmates looked up from their sewing or reading to call a greeting as she passed.

Roberto was seated at the desk in the last cell which was reserved for the MRTA library. He was reading the current issue of a Peruvian news magazine as she entered, and he jumped up to give her a tight bearhug and a kiss on the forehead.

"Sit down." He urged her onto the chair he had occupied." Tell me what's new in the *barrio* and what mischief my nephews have gotten into since last week."

"I'll get to that in a minute," she promised, "but first, I brought you these things." She pulled out the cigarettes, trousers, undershirt, and handkerchief, and, finally, the tennis shoes. "And there's a message from Pedro taped into the left sole under the cloth lining. He wants me to bring the answer back when I leave, so you'd better show it to Rodrigo now."

CHAPTER 3

The first Canto Grande tunnel was started by the MRTA political prisoners in May 1987, despite extremely adverse conditions.

A circular subterranean corridor beneath the central patio of the penitentiary provided prison guards with access to each of the six pavilions. This was intended as a riot-control measure in the event that prisoners tried to barricade themselves inside one or more of the prison blocks. Beneath that corridor are the sewage ducts of the prison, emptying into an escape-proof outlet. Access doors to the pavilions and to the ducts are always securely locked, but by early 1987 the MRTA had obtained duplicate keys through means they were reluctant to discuss with us and had explored the underground reaches of the prison and decided where to make their escape attempt.

The tunnel mouth was located in the side wall of the concrete sewage duct, approximately forty meters from the entrance and beneath one of the other pavilions so that in case of discovery no suspicion would fall on the inmates of 2-A. Three shifts of prisoners set to work on the tunnel. Jaime formed part of the shift from 10 to 12 noon. Another group worked from 8 p.m. to 1:30 a.m., while the third took over from 1:30 until 5.

The tunnel was little more than a rabbit hole, some sixty centimeters high by fifty centimeters wide. One man would dig, scooping the loose dirt back between his legs, while a second collected it in a sack and backed out to the entrance where a third would scatter the contents of the sack along the bottom of the slimy canal. The hole was too small to turn around in, and the only illumination was provided by flashlights. Despite the three shifts of diggers, the work went slowly and the tunnel advanced at the snail's pace of two meters per week.

None of the diggers had any experience in tunneling, nor did they have access to timbers with which to shore up the roof of the tunnel to prevent cave-ins. Difficulties in disposing of the earth they excavated dictated the cramped dimensions of the tunnel. In the early stages, they hauled sacks of earth up into the underground corridor and from there to the patio of Pavilion 2-A, where they scattered it in the patio itself. One of the diggers carelessly left the rope used to raise the sacks in the sewage duct, and it was discovered by prison guards during one of their routine inspection patrols. This alerted prison authorities to the fact that an escape attempt was underway, but they were unable to locate the tunnel entrance. Teams of guards began hammering the earth in the patio in an effort to detect the hollow reverberations a tunnel would give off, but they were equally unsuccessful.

Work on the tunnel continued, and the dirt was spread in a thin layer on the floor of the sewage channel itself.

Each morning at 9:30 a civil employee of the prison entered the underground corridor and used one of the access gates to climb up to the roof of the pavilion where the main water tank was located. He turned on the valves that distributed running water to the different pavilions and returned the way he had come. The MRTA prisoners were aware of this daily routine and didn't start digging until half an hour after he had left.

On 14 July 1967, however, he unexpectedly returned shortly after 10, climbed up to the water tank again — perhaps to open a valve he had overlooked — and when he returned, he heard strange noises issuing from the sewage duct. The manhole was unlocked and open, and he climbed down into the duct itself to investigate, but was unable to discern anything in the pitch darkness. The third man on the excavation team, however, saw him outlined against the light from the corridor above and gave the alarm signal. The diggers hastily blocked the tunnel entrance and made their way back to Pavilion 2-A. Nothing unusual occurred during the rest of the day, and that night Jaime and two others scouted the duct again and attempted to conceal the entrance to the tunnel.

The next day was a Wednesday — visitors' day — and the prison guards were kept busy with the influx. On Thursday, the 16th, however, prison authorities launched a full-scale search for the tunnel and discovered the entrance. By then, the tunnel had only advanced twenty meters and was still well within the prison walls.

Lima newspapers carried the story of the discovery the following day, and prison authorities made a show of rounding up suspected ringleaders, isolating them in punishment cells and beating them soundly while interrogating them. Common prisoners on the second and third floors of Pavilion 2-A were among those questioned, but only five of the MRTA prisoners were singled out for questioning, and none of them admitted anything.

The Directorate of the MRTA followed the progress of this first escape effort attentively, and when it aborted they immediately held an evaluation session to analyze the mistakes that had led to the discovery of the tunnel. They came to the conclusion that it was virtually impossible for the MRTA prisoners to construct a successful escape tunnel from inside the prison. It was highly unlikely that proper digging tools and the other material required could be smuggled into Canto Grande without discovery, and even if that could be achieved, there was no safe way of getting rid of the dirt within the prison walls.

There is no record of who experienced the flash of illumination that inverted the terms of the problem: "If the *compañeros* can't dig their way out of Canto Grande, why don't we dig our way in and bring them out?"

That this decision was discussed and approved immediately after the first project collapsed is demonstrated by the fact that only eleven days after Jaime's release he was assigned to the team that would undertake the second dig. Five senior militants of the organization were assigned to work full-time on the planning and execution of the rescue attempt.

Nestor, one of the senior members of the MRTA in terms of age and experience, was a member of the Central Committee and privy to the progress of the planning, though he did not participate directly in the first stage, since his responsibility at that time was to create MRTA guerrilla groups in the Andes and find ways to support them logistically.

By mid-1987 — he tells us — we had a growing number of *compañeros* in Canto Grande. The decision was made at the highest level to try to rescue them. A planning group set to work, but during the six months from July to the end of the year a series of obstacles and unforeseen circumstances prevented the project from making any headway.

The first order of business for the planners was to find a suitable location as close to the prison as possible from which to start the dig. Scouting expeditions to the Canto Grande area soon made it clear that the only viable sites were five vacant lots within a few hundred meters of the prison wall. All of these were owned by a *Señor* Aldaña and discreet inquiries revealed that they were for sale.

The MRTA planners selected a middle-aged couple of militants — "Uncle Felix" and his wife — to pose as buyers, and chose Antonio, who had been charged with on-site responsibility for the dig, to pose as their son. Uncle Felix was a master mason with years of experience in construction work, and it was he who drew up the plans for the safe house that would serve as the excavation site.

The three of them called on Aldaña and learned that the lots were indeed for sale, but at a very steep price. Aldaña expressed surprise at the visit and asked:

"How did you know I was selling?"

Uncle Felix explained that they had made inquiries of the neighbors who suggested that they contact Aldaña. Put off by the high price, Felix said he needed time to think it over, and they left to consult the MRTA planners.

The MRTA told him to make a show of bargaining to drive the price down, but to go ahead with the purchase and start construction of the safe house as soon as possible. Felix returned and signed the sales contract, but when he and Antonio set off to buy building materials, they discovered there was no cement to be had in the country. The government had bought up existing supplies for the construction of an electric railway system. This shortage cost them a month's delay, but they finally purchased the starting materials and began laying the foundation and raising the brick walls.

It was during this period that guerrillas of the MRTA took the town of Concua in the Andes. In reaction to this event, the Canto Grande authorities increased security measures as a precaution against a possible external attack on the prison itself, and they also sent out security patrols to take a census of individuals who lived in the area.

I arrived early with another *compañero* who was a friend of mine — Antonio recalls — and we had started mixing sand and concrete to get on with the job when Uncle Felix arrived on the scene. Two Republican guards were talking to *Señor* Aldaña, who called to Felix:

"Come over here a minute, neighbor; they're asking for our documents."

Uncle Felix gave the guards the number of his electoral identification document, and one of them asked to see it. He scrutinized it closely, suspiciously, and copied down the data on it. Uncle Felix had made the mistake of giving his wife's surname as the same as his own instead of using her maiden name.

The problem was that both Felix and his wife were using false documentation, and he stumbled instead of answering questions glibly. The guards moved on to the next house to continue their census taking, and nothing untoward happened. Antonio insisted that they all remain at the building site for another hour instead of arousing suspicions by leaving immediately, but as soon as he returned to Lima, he reported the incident to his MRTA superiors. They analyzed the situation carefully and decided that the half-built house had to be abandoned. The tunnel project was too important to permit it to be threatened by a basic security error. The whole enterprise could collapse if the guard who had taken the data simply checked it against central identity records.

The Directorate decided that Antonio should liquidate the first site, and that the "owners" of the second site, still to be acquired, must purchase it in their true names and have legal documentation to back up their identities.

Antonio returned to the house site several days later and spoke with a neighbor lady who lived across the street. Everything appeared normal, but he did not want to speak to Aldaña. He explained to her that an urgent family problem had arisen, and that he and his parents had to return to Arequipa immediately. He asked her to explain the situation to Aldaña and to please keep an eye on the unfinished house until his family could return, which of course they never would.

That terminated Phase One of the Canto Grande tunnel project. The Directorate began a search for a new set of "owners" and safe-house keepers who would be strictly legal. It was November 1987. Six months had gone by, and no progress whatsoever had been made.

CHAPTER 4

It was during this hiatus that two members of the MRTA Directorate were captured, sentenced, and remanded to Canto Grande. This seriously weakened the command structure of the organization. Nestor, who had fulfilled his assignment and turned the day-to-day task of running the guerrilla networks over to other cadres, was now charged with responsibility for the tunnel project.

A young, unmarried couple whose identity documents were in order had been assigned to purchase another of *Señor* Aldaña's lots, start construction of a second safe house, and move in as safe-house keepers when it was habitable. The man was given the pseudonym of "the Goth" (*el gótico*). His companion was a young girl — only nineteen years old — and neither of them had had any previous clandestine experience nor had they been tested and proven as disciplined revolutionary militants. The Goth was told that he and his girlfriend were being assigned an important task that would take from two to four months to complete, after which he could return to his previous occupation — a job that had certain cultural connotations.

Despite the setbacks and frustrations that marked the first phase of the project, the individuals assigned to carry it out were strongly motivated, enthusiastic, and, because of their inexperience, wildly over-optimistic. All of them were confident that once the safe house had been erected and the excavation started, the tunnel itself could be completed within a few months.

The Goth agreed to undertake this relatively short-term assignment, but demanded a salary to support himself and his *compañera*. The organization agreed to this, and he went surreptitiously with a member of the planning team to select one of the remaining lots. Both Antonio and Uncle Felix were "burned" and couldn't appear openly in the neighborhood inasmuch as they were supposed to be in Arequipa. The planner chose an inconspicuous site and sent the couple to negotiate the purchase with *Señor* Aldaña. They discovered that Aldaña had only one lot left for sale: it was directly behind the commercial sandpit, and it also happened to be the one closest to the prison and in clear view of the guards in Tower No. 8. It was a security risk that had to be accepted: as the Spanish saying has it, "Necessity has the face of a dog."

The Goth hired a construction contractor and gave him the plans Uncle Felix had prepared; the contractor promised that the walls would be up and the house roofed within thirty days.

By January 1988 one room was habitable, and the couple moved in. By this time the tunnel planners had revised their earlier estimate of how long it would take to dig a tunnel more than 300 meters in length and came up with a new timetable for completing the project: six months. When they heard the news, the Goth and his girlfriend complained bitterly that they had been deceived. They had been promised that they would have to take care of the house for a maximum of four months.

Worse still, no one had informed them of the true nature of the project. The daring plan to tunnel into Canto Grande was highly sensitive information, and from the beginning, was kept carefully compartmented within the MRTA. With a team of diggers due to move into the safe house within a few weeks, the planners decided that it was time to inform the caretakers, and it fell to Antonio to reveal the full details to them.

When he explained the importance of the project and stressed the tight security measures that would be necessary throughout its execution, the Goth's face fell, and Antonio sensed that he didn't like the situation in which he found himself a single bit. Antonio and the others had assumed that, as an MRTA militant, the Goth would willingly accept orders and run whatever risks were necessary to carry out a task the organization deemed of vital importance. But he had already proven himself to be balky and of dubious reliability.

While the house was being constructed, he and Antonio held regular operational meetings in a Lima café, but he was frequently late, with the lame excuse that he had been delayed by friends. A few weeks earlier, Antonio had given him funds and told him to go out and buy a secondhand car the following day. This would be the project's only operational vehicle and would ostensibly serve as a taxi, with the Goth posing as a taxi driver. The Goth shook his head and said it wouldn't be possible because he had made arrangements to go to the beach with his parents. Antonio observed that revolutionary discipline took precedence over personal pleasure, and that he should cancel his beach excursion, but the Goth argued that it was the last time he would have a chance to be with his parents before being cooped up in the safe house for a lengthy period. The upshot was that he and his girlfriend went to the beach and the taxi purchase was delayed until the following week. The vehicle he bought for 1000 dollars was a venerable Dodge four-door sedan which was never entirely trouble-free.

Even before that, Antonio now recalled, as soon as the lot purchase had been concluded, he had told the Goth to go out and find a contractor to start work on the house. The Goth demurred, saying he would get around to that the following day because he had an important lunch date with friends.

Things apparently went smoothly for some weeks. The caretakers moved into the unfinished house and started getting acquainted with the neighbors. The MRTA planners decided to wait for a discreet interval before the team of diggers moved in and set to work. This would permit the couple to get acclimated and avoid complications in case the Canto Grande authorities decided to submit new residents to a security check and, possibly, a house search. Antonio couldn't appear openly at the safe house and continued to meet with the Goth in Lima. The latter invariably assured him that everything was fine and that they were well received in the neighborhood.

The Directorate, however, decided to send out one of its members to make an independent check. He discovered that some of the neighbors suspected that the couple were drug traffickers. Why? Because the Goth had been giving away bricks he had purchased for the house construction, and nobody in their right mind gives away bricks unless they have more money than they know what to do with. Also, the local carpenter was impressed with the affluence of his new neighbors. He had installed some doors and window frames for them, and now he had nearly talked them into letting him build them an expensive set of dining room furniture.

At their next meeting, Antonio reprimanded the Goth for these actions. The latter felt aggrieved that the organization was spying on him, and as for the gift of bricks, he said, he was merely trying to ingratiate himself with the neighbors, as he had been instructed to do. And what was wrong with having a decent set of dining room furniture?

The construction workers who had built the house finished plastering the walls and left. The MRTA instructed Antonio and another member to move into the safe house and start work on the tunnel itself. Antonio had to arrive clandestinely, crouched in the back seat of the taxi with a plastic sheet over him, while the Goth got out, opened the iron gate and drove into the high-walled patio. The wall surrounding the house had been built especially high to keep the prison guards in Tower No. 8 from spying on their every movement, and particularly on the comings and goings of the car.

Sewage lines had not yet been opened in the Canto Grande area, and the occupants of the safe house used an outdoor, Chick Sales two-hole latrine in the patio. Uncle Felix took this fact into account in designing the house plans with an internal bathroom that would not be used until the sewage system was installed. The toilet was of the Turkish type: a square sheet of metal set into the floor with a circular opening in the center and two raised footprints to stand on. This, in fact, was to be the entrance to the tunnel. The porcelainized metal sheet was hinged and could be swung up to the rear wall and secured to reveal the vertical shaft.

Neither Antonio nor his companion had any construction or excavation experience, but they set to work with a will, digging down four meters and then starting a horizontal shaft under the house, leading toward the vacant lots across the street.

Problems cropped up immediately. The Goth's girlfriend was flighty and undisciplined, and she frequently didn't have lunch ready until 4 p.m., which did nothing to ingratiate her with the hungry diggers. The Goth himself didn't participate in the digging. His job was to haul away sacks of dirt in the morning, then buy whatever construction materials were needed for the immediate future and return home by noon to load the old red taxi with more sacks of dirt. Once the digging started he was forbidden to associate with his old friends for security reasons, and he was supposed to adhere to a regular schedule of comings and goings. Instead, it was soon discovered that he was telephoning and visiting his friends in Lima and that he failed to adhere to the agreed schedule, with the consequence that the dirt piled up. When Antonio asked him to haul away an additional five sacks, he complained that it was too heavy a load for the ancient vehicle. Finally, in complete contravention of security rules, the couple would take off in the Dodge while Antonio and his companion were digging, and leave the safe house abandoned.

Antonio and the planning task force were imbued with the importance of the task at hand and the necessity of carrying it out in a disciplined way, whereas the couple took it as an irksome imposition on their personal lives and consistently placed their own convenience ahead of the demands of the job they had undertaken. Antonio had to exercise tact and friendly persuasion in an attempt to integrate the two of them into the working group. The core of the problem lay in the fact that the Goth was indispensable, and he knew it. The house was in his name. The Dodge taxi and the construction materials were purchased in his name, and the couple had been made privy to the details of the project. They were both unhappy that the job would stretch out longer than they had been promised, and they made their feelings apparent by shirking their responsibilities and engaging in slowdown tactics. Their slackness slowed the work of the diggers to a snail's pace and created personal frictions on both sides. A month after Antonio started to work, only the vertical shaft and a few meters of tunnel had been excavated and the MRTA Directorate was growing impatient at the lack of progress. Nestor decided to intervene personally and arranged a meeting in Lima with Antonio and the Goth.

In the first place — Nestor told us — I feel that we made a poor evaluation when we selected the couple: two youngsters who hadn't spent much time in organizational party life. They began displaying a totally negative attitude, and the *compañeros* working on the tunnel were unable to make much progress.

Nestor and Antonio explained once again the importance of the tunnel project and stressed that each of the participants had to fulfill his share of the responsibility punctually so that the work could go forward smoothly.

We even told him — Antonio recalls — that he was part of a huge machine, one of a group of dedicated friends, but if he couldn't pull his weight we would have to replace him with somebody else. I realize that's an authoritarian concept, but we put it to him in that way so he would do some serious thinking. We did it to shake him up and get his feet on the ground, but he kept on making problems, more convinced than ever that now, with the lot purchased and the house already built, we couldn't turn back and, more than ever, he was indispensable.

The Directorate recognized that a basic reason for the slow progress was that neither Antonio nor the other digger had any construction experience, so on 23 May 1988 they sent Jaime and Uncle Felix to join the digging crew. The latter immediately saw that the house had to be soundproofed. The safe house was ostensibly occupied only by the Goth and his "wife," but there were already four diggers living there clandestinely, with more to come.

Uncle Felix and Jaime set about filling in chinks in the walls and stuccoing them so passersby could not overhear six different voices or the sounds of excavation when work began on the tunnel itself. The only place for the diggers to hide in the event of a surprise inspection by the Republicans was in the tunnel itself, which was uncomfortably cramped, so the entrance to the tunnel at the bottom of the vertical shaft had to be enlarged. A new bathroom also had to be constructed in the patio to replace the primitive latrine.

These reforms were accomplished by the beginning of July, and the diggers were able for the first time to concentrate on the tunnel itself. This was another rabbit hole, with dimensions only a bit larger than those of the first tunnel from inside Canto Grande. Jaime's experience with that dig was accepted by the others as valid, and it seemed obvious to all that a larger tunnel would take longer to dig and would require the removal of much more dirt than the ancient taxi could accommodate.

Even with a total of four diggers, progress continued to be painfully slow, and in August the Directorate sent Armando to the safe house to find out what was going wrong.

Armando is a technician who knows tunnels and tunneling. He had been engaged in other activities for the MRTA and was previously unable to participate in the Canto Grande project. His arrival on the scene, according to Antonio, had all the impact of an earthquake.

When the technician arrived, he made us see that our ideas were an unrealizable Utopia. In the first place, the tunnel had to be much larger. We were digging a hole that measured eighty by fifty centimeters, and he told us it had to be at least one meter forty by seventy centimeters.

"With those dimensions, how much dirt will we have to move?" we asked him. He took out his pocket calculator, started pressing buttons and came up with an answer that horrified us. A pile of dirt as tall as the house would have to be hauled away every week.

"But the old Dodge won't be able to handle that much," I objected. "It can only carry about ten sacks a day."

"In that case," he replied, "we'll have to look for something bigger."

Jaime smiled with satisfaction at that last remark. Armando looked around at the cramped bathroom and shook his head.

"This will never do," he told the others. "There's not enough working space in here, or down below either. Let's see the rest of the house."

He, Antonio, Uncle Felix, and Jaime made an inspection of the three-bedroom structure. Armando stopped in the back bedroom, looked it over carefully and made up his mind.

"This is where we start," he said.

"Start?" Antonio echoed, "But we've already started. We have ten meters of tunnel we can enlarge."

Armando shrugged resignedly.

"We'll have to abandon that and start over from here," he told them. "We'll build a false wall across the room, have a closet door here and start the tunnel shaft behind the wall."

The four of them returned to the living-dining room and sat down at the modest unpainted table where they were joined by the Goth. Antonio was still dazed by the revolutionary overturn of all their plans and expectations.

"Well," he finally said, "with all these changes and having to start over again on a much larger scale, how long do you think it will take us to finish the job?"

Armando leaned back and gazed at the ceiling for several long moments.

"If everything goes smoothly," he said, "it will take at least eight months to a year."

The Goth gasped, sputtered and exploded like a string of firecrackers.

CHAPTER 5

When Ciro arrived at Canto Grande at the end of 1986, while the maximum-security regime was still in force, it was impossible for the MRTA political prisoners to engage in group activities or develop a sense of collective identity, but they were able to pass written messages back and forth between the cells and to engage in brief snatches of conversation in the patio.

Different pressures were at work to gradually modify the prison system, however. One of the most traumatic of these took place in mid-1986.

In the early morning of June 18, while an international conference of Social Democratic parties was taking place in Lima, prison riots planned and coordinated by the *Sendero Luminoso* broke out in three separate prisons in the Lima area: "*El Frontón*" located on an island facing Lima; the "Santa Barbara" women's prison in Callao, and the Lurigancho prison on the northeastern outskirts of the capital. Some 375 *Senderistas* rebelled simultaneously in the different prisons. They managed to take over some of the pavilions and prison installations: captured a number of hostages and presented a joint petition demanding improvements in their living conditions, including a decent diet and medical attention. They also demanded to be recognized as political prisoners, or in their terms, "prisoners of war." At no time did the rioters attempt to break out of jail, nor did the prison authorities at any point lose physical control of the situation.

The Council of Ministers immediately decided to crush the uprising. They placed the armed forces in charge of suppressing the riots and limited their directive for accomplishing this to the recommendation that "insofar as possible, the lives of the hostages should be respected." How the rioters themselves were to be reduced was not mentioned. No serious attempts were made to negotiate with the rioters, absolute censorship was imposed, and newsmen were barred from the areas.

The Navy took over *"El Frontón,"* the army moved into Lurigancho, the Air Force took responsibility for "Santa Barbara," and 36 hours later 248 of the rioters were dead in a massacre unprecedented in recent Peruvian history. There were no survivors in Lurigancho, approximately 50 out of 179 in *"El Frontón,"* whereas in "Santa Barbara," only two women died and another later committed suicide: a clear indicator that the situation could have been controlled with less violence in the other two prisons.

An investigating committee headed by a Senator was established and eventually issued a moderately condemnatory report that spoke of "excesses," but was essentially a whitewash. Nevertheless, the bloody episode registered in the Peruvian collective unconscious, and in its wake prison authorities modified their previous reliance on physical brutality and the naked use of force to compel obedience in the prisons.

The unanticipated explosion of the prison population also forced a modification of the strict "lockup" regime. Two double bunks of concrete were installed in each cell, but to confine four individuals in suchlimited space created intolerable strains, and eventually the cell doors in each block had to be left open so the prisoners could spill out into the single wide corridor running the length of each pavilion.

Little by little — Ciro told us — sabotage became systematic. Not only we, but the common prisoners, began destroying the built-in locks. It became impossible to maintain the maximum security regime, and the time arrived when the prisoners could move normally in each pavilion day and night. This was a more favorable situation for us, because we could go on talking, hold meetings, and carry on activities at any hour. This enabled us to consolidate an *esprit de corps*, to work to overcome personal weaknesses in each *compañero*, help each other in different ways and attain a position of firmness and strength. We planned an agenda of daily activities for a three-month period, after which we developed a more advanced 90-day plan.

Ernesto was another of the "old hands" at Canto Grande. The son of a peasant family from Piura, he was studying medicine at San Marcos University in Lima when his girl friend recruited him for the MRTA in 1984. His schooling proved too costly for his family to sustain, and that year he dropped out of the university to devote full time to urban guerrilla activities. During 1985 and 1986, he participated in armed propaganda activities and the taking of radio stations to broadcast MRTA pronouncements.

On March 28, 1987, at the beginning of the school year, he was engaged in an operation to hold up a shoe store and distribute shoes to needy students. The operation was successful, but when Ernesto mingled with the crowd to make his getaway, a store employee followed him and pointed him out to the police. A shootout ensued at the Central Market in front of the Ministry of Economy. When Ernesto ran out of ammunition, he took to his heels with three policemen after him. As luck would have it, he ran full tilt into a fat policeman who detained him. The others came up, arrested and handcuffed him and took him in a taxi to police headquarters. The two police on either side of him in the back seat started interrogating him. When he refused to answer them, the policeman in the front seat flew into a rage, drew his gun, turned around and deliberately shot Ernesto twice. One of the bullets pierced his lung and liver and lodged in his spine, where it remains to this day. The other bullet perforated his intestines. He remained conscious while they took him to the hospital and finally operated on him at 11 p.m. He was sewed together with 20 stitches, spent two days in coma and 24 days in the hospital.

DIRCOTE wanted to interrogate him, but the doctors said no. His family traced him, and because of his physical condition he was not tortured but turned over to the Ministry of Justice instead, and on April 25, he was remanded to Canto Grande.

Ernesto described the daily routine of the MRTA prisoners as follows:

Reveille was at 0600 hours, and the first activity was one hour of setting up exercises in the corridor. At 0700, they assembled in military formation, raised the MRTA flag and sang the party hymn. This was followed by a chorus of slogans pertaining to the political situation of the nation or slogans of protest against prison conditions they were determined to reform. After this, one of the group read news bulletins that had been picked up on the radio or had appeared in the daily newspapers, and comments on the news were invited from all hands.

After breakfast, each cell was cleaned by its inhabitants and a rotating group swept and mopped the communal living space of the pavilion corridor while a cooking detail set about preparing lunch.

Security was a constant preoccupation in Pavilion 2-A. The pavilion entrance was chained and padlocked during the night, and sentries armed with knives guarded the entrance during the day.

When Ciro arrived at Canto Grande, there were 13 political prisoners of the MRTA already in residence, and approximately 40 *Senderistas*. By the time they started digging the first tunnel, the MRTA population had increased to 30, and when that project failed, the National Directorate decided to make a full-scale effort to free them.

For Ciro and Ernesto, 1987 was a year of apprenticeship and adjustment to prison life. The common prisoners in Canto Grande were for the most part hardened criminals, some with six or seven convictions behind them, and learning to deal with them was an education in itself.

It's a very special way of life — Ernesto told us — and basically it implies two things: first of all, strength, or having the capability of defending oneself against any form of aggression, and secondly, having the political capability to deal with those people. You have to know how to combine both factors, because if you think they're going to respect you simply because you're a political prisoner, you'll soon learn that isn't so. They sneer at you and take you for a fool. They'll only respect you once they learn that you have the strength and the political organizing ability to stand up to them.

Most of us had never so much as seen the inside of a police station, and suddenly we found ourselves inside a maximum security detention center designed for the most hardened, most dangerous, criminals. It was a reality we had never imagined, but we started learning from our bruises, literally, because there were fist-fights. So, internally we started developing a much more solid and cohesive organizational life. We organized schools for the formation of cadres, for political and ideological formation. We carried out cultural activities and formed musical groups with primitive instruments — the drum, for example, was a plastic bucket — but with a great desire to make music, and we finally reached the point where we taped two cassettes of near professional quality in which the music and the lyrics

were of our own composition. We also had a theater group
that gave performances for family members on visitor's
days. With the help of some family members we formed a
literary study group, and we even had a poetry workshop.

Afternoons were dedicated to "collective labor:" the MRTA
prisoners started working with straw, weaving purses,
baskets and hats, which their family members sold outside
the prison. They branched out to the manufacture of jute
rugs, the production of greeting cards for Christmas, New
Year's, wedding anniversaries and birthdays. Leather work
was another major money maker, and some members of the
group specialized in wallets, purses and even shoes. A
carpentry shop was established on the ground floor where
the prisoners made tables, chairs and trays for their own use
as well as for sale. The income from these productive
activities went a long way toward defraying each prisoner's
extra expenses, particularly because family members sold
them at "solidarity" prices.

Ernesto explained the ulterior objectives of all these
activities, which were planned and encouraged by the
internal MRTA leaders:

The primary objective of every prisoner is, of course, to
recover his freedom. But as time goes by and the awareness
sinks in that escape is virtually impossible, secondary
objectives take form. First of all, we were determined to
convert Canto Grande into another trench of the liberation
struggle, and secondly, to take advantage of the time we had
to spend in prison to the integral formation of each
compañero: to dedicating ourselves to the creation of the
"new man" that Che talks about, in each one of us. The
"new man" is not merely an ideologist or political animal,
nor only a Marxist-Leninist, but a man of broader
formation with the capability of understanding the world
around him in an integrated way. We felt that part of this

was physical education, and that, besides the political and ideological education we received, our experience in collective labor and our cultural and artistic formation were also of primary importance.

"What was your relationship with the Republican prison guards?" we asked Ernesto.

We were very clear about the fact that the ordinary enlisted men — the wardens we dealt with every day — were not our principal enemy. They are part of the people, who enlisted in the belief that they were defending their country and in order to have a decent standard of living. We felt no prejudices or animosity toward them. Our basic objective was to try to neutralize them, and occasionally to try to give them a bit of political education, making them see what their function was within the existing system, making them understand that their relationship with us didn't necessarily have to be a conflictive one. We respect the laws of war. In practice, we have demonstrated that: when the *compañeros* take a town in the jungle, we have been respectful toward the policemen who surrender. The prison guards differentiated between us and the *Sendero Luminoso* prisoners who follow a different set of rules.

The MRTA prisoners actively cultivated friendly relations with the prison guards, and in the process they managed to accumulate important intelligence information on the internal workings of the prison system: what were their hours on duty and when did the guard shifts change; details of the internal security system; what were the relations between the officers and subalterns; what type of armaments existed inside the prison and who was allowed to carry weapons. The ordinary prison guard, or turnkey, for example, was unarmed except for a nightstick. The guards on duty in the eight towers were armed with automatic combat rifles and had authority to fire on anything that moved in the free-fire zones on either side of the main prison wall. And, of course, there was a carefully-guarded arsenal that could be opened if needed.

The political prisoners collected and hoarded such scraps of information and passed it on to their internal leaders. They didn't know why they were encouraged to do this nor how the information would eventually be put to use, but they had faith that the day would come when all these interwoven bits and pieces of intelligence about the inner workings of Canto Grande would prove to be important.

THE TIME TUNNEL-II

José Gabriel Túpac Amaru was a direct descendant of Inca Túpac Amaru and proud of his royal heritage. In the course of his education, he was influenced by the European Enlightenment. As a local *cacique*, or chieftain, he waged a continuing legal battle against the pitiless Spanish exploitation of the Indian masses in Peru.

When he rose in rebellion in November 1780, thousands of Indians, responding to the charisma of his name and ancient rank as well as to the liberating content of his message, flocked to his cause, and turbulent uprisings succeeded each other throughout the entire area once ruled by the Inca empire.

A wily political strategist, Túpac Amaru took care not to challenge the Spanish crown or the Catholic Church directly. In addition to the mass following of his own indigenous peoples, he sought to enlist under his banner the *criollos* (Peruvians of Spanish descent); the *mestizo* population of mixed Spanish-Indian blood; the negroes and mulattos, to whom he promised abolition of slavery. He was careful to avoid the word, "independence," just as he avoided taking a position with respect to expropriation of the vast *latifundios* owned by the elite of Spanish descent.

Instead, he aimed his fire at the *corregidores*, the provincial governors of the colonial regime, who were notorious for their greed, corruption and heartless squeezing of the indigenous population. He condemned forced labor in the mines and *obrajes*, or primitive textile factories, which was imposed by the Spanish overlords as annual tribute to the Spanish crown. There can be no doubt, however, that his eventual objective was liberation from Spain and restoration of the former Inca empire.

As a military strategist, he was less able; he might have captured Cuzco had he struck promptly before Spanish reinforcements arrived. Eventually, Spanish forces surrounded and besieged his forces, and Túpac Amaru himself was captured on April 6, 1781. He remained silent under torture and, after being forced to watch the garroting of his wife and able confederate, Micaela Bastidas, and their two children, he himself was drawn and quartered in the public plaza of Cuzco. When the four wiry Andean ponies, between which he was suspended in mid-air, failed to sunder his body, he was beheaded as an act of compassion: the same fate which his forebear, Inca Túpac Amaru, had suffered at the hands of the Spanish conquerors 210 years earlier.

CHAPTER 6

After the initial shock wore off, the diggers were enthused by the technological solution Armando had imposed on them, even though it roughly quadrupled the work that had to be accomplished. The first step — building a false wall across the back bedroom — not only provided a secure entrance to the tunnel shaft, but also muffled the sounds of excavation and created a space where the sacks of earth could be stored until they were hauled away. The entrance itself was a rectangular vertical shaft measuring 1 meter by 80 centimeters and five meters deep. The sides were cemented, and the rungs of the vertical ladder were set into the cement.

Once again they started excavating horizontally toward the vacant lots across the street, their digging tools limited to pointed hardwood sticks, padded at the end to muffle the noise of hammer blows. Armando wanted the dimensions to be 1.50 meters high by 1 meter wide, but this met with spirited opposition from the diggers, and he finally negotiated a compromise with the team: the tunnel would be 1.25 meters high by 80 centimeters wide. These dimensions would permit two persons to move past each other, and the shaft would be wide enough for the eventual installation of mine cars to carry away the sacks of earth.

Another major difference from the previous tunnels was that this time the horizontal shaft was timbered from the beginning to prevent cave-ins. Approximately every two meters, vertical timbers of eucalyptus wood were installed and capped with a crossbeam of the same material. Then wooden planks were strung from one crossbeam to the next and the earthen ceiling of the tunnel itself was supported by rocks wedged in between it and the planks. On the previous tunnel, Uncle Felix had improvised an anti-cave-in system by splashing the walls and ceiling with a stucco cement mixture that, when dry, held the overhead sand and dirt in place. Now the diggers continued using this system between the timbers of the shoring system wherever pockets of crumbling sand made it advisable.

An underground shower was installed so the diggers could wash up after their shifts, and the waste water from this was collected and used to damp down the tunnel face. This eliminated much of the dust from the digging, cooled the air to lower the temperature in the shaft and, according to Jaime, the water gave off oxygen and refreshed the nostrils and lungs of the diggers as they worked.

Electric wires were strung from one crossbeam to the next, and 25-watt bulbs illuminated the tunnel at periodic intervals, while the diggers at the far end worked with brighter lights.

When the new horizontal shaft had advanced a short distance, it converged with the previous tunnel from the safe-house bathroom, which was now enlarged to conform to the new dimensions. Armando inspected the point of convergence contentedly.

"This wasn't a wasted effort after all," he told the others, "because it will help solve our ventilation problem."

Not only that, but the space where the two shafts met was enlarged and squared off to form a small underground salon which also housed the bookshelves of the collective library, while the underground shower was located in an alcove a few meters further on.

With four diggers working from 0800 to 1700, except for a two-hour break for lunch, the work went slowly because of the many large rocks that had to be removed, and the tunnel advanced at the snail's pace of 30 to 40 centimeters per day. Still, after the months of frustration and forced inactivity, this seemed a heartening change. The Canto Grande project was finally moving forward.

The housekeeping couple, however, continued to sour relations at the operational site. The Goth had raised a verbal storm when he learned the new time schedule for completing the project. Antonio recalls the deepening crisis in these words:

When the technician told us that the job couldn't be finished in three or four months but would take at least eight months to a year, the couple thought that was horrible. The fact is that the Goth had been traumatized from the very first days after they moved into the safe-house. He returned late one night — which he wasn't supposed to do — and one of the tower guards fired a warning shot in the air. Another pair of guards came to the house some minutes later and told him to report to the prison commandant the following morning with his identity documents, because he was new in the neighborhood and they wanted to know more about him.

The next morning, when he complained about the gunshot, the commandant told him he should thank God he was still alive, because the tower guards had orders to shoot to kill. This episode convinced the Goth that the *Republicanos* were suspicious of him and were keeping him under observation. Then when he learned what the safe-house was to be used for, he became literally crazed with fear and started deliberately creating problems in order to be relieved of his dangerous assignment.

Jaime, pugnacious and short-tempered by nature, had had enough of the couple's systematic sabotage. The final straw came one evening when the pair invited guests in during the afternoon. The four diggers left off work and showered at

1700 before they became aware of what was happening upstairs. They had no choice but to remain at the bottom of the shaft until the intruders left. The hours ticked by, dinner-time came and went, and the Gothic couple continued chatting imperturbably with their visitors while the diggers below ground fumed and grew famished. This was a deliberate provocation and a flouting of all the rules of comradeliness. When the visitors finally left after midnight and there was no dinner prepared for the workers, Jaime blew up and told the Goth that if such a thing were to happen on a guerrilla front in the jungle, the Goth would be taken out and shot.

Jaime went too far — Antonio tells us — and we criticized him for it, because in the first place it wasn't up to him to make threats — not even the project director had talked to him that way — and the Goth seized on this incident and converted it into an argument in his favor.

"Nobody is motivated to do a job because he is going to be killed," he said. "I can't go on this way when at any minute somebody might stick a knife in my back."

It made me mad — Antonio admits — because it was the best reason he had come up with to argue that he couldn't keep on working with us. But in any case it would have been better for him to leave, because at any moment the whole situation could explode.

The tensions within the safe-house reached such a pitch that the National Directorate felt it necessary to call a meeting to air the grievances on both sides and decide how to resolve the impasse. At the meeting, the Goth was by turns defensive and aggressive. He accused the others of mistreating him and found excuses, as usual, for each of his own misdeeds. When the other members of the team pressed him, he stood up angrily and said:

"I'm going to get out of here. I can't keep on working at this job."

The members of the Directorate lectured him sternly, and once more he backed down and promised that he would start cooperating in the project and be on his good behavior from then on. But, as Antonio explains wearily, within a few days he was up to his old tricks:

Anyway, we returned to the safe-house and went back to work, but every time he brought in a *compañero* in the car, he displayed a reckless attitude to intimidate them — as if he were capable of driving right up to the prison gates and have them arrested, or as if to tell them, "You'd better watch your step around me." On one occasion when he brought a *compañero* to the house at 2 in the morning, with the other lying in the back seat covered with a plastic sheet, he stopped the car near the house, got out and abandoned the man for 15 minutes, presumably to take a leak. But it was a clear-cut provocation.

I came back to the house after that, and they told me what had been going on. It was incredible that only a few days after displaying a more self-critical attitude, he had now shifted to an attitude of direct provocation and was deliberately trying to create problems. At that point I began thinking that he'd gone out of his mind, because his acts were clearly abnormal; they were desperate efforts on his part to get out of the situation in which he found himself.

The couple began showing up late every day: once it was because they'd had an accident; the next day they had run into a drunk; the day after that they'd been stopped and taken to the police station. A series of transparent lies. Something or other went wrong every day.

There were other aggravations as well. They had a mangy little dog that the girl would bathe in the kitchen sink where she washed the dishes. The dog got sick and she closed him up in the room where the diggers slept on the floor.

To top things off, Jaime, who was furious with both of them, found a notebook one day on the living room table. He opened it and leafed through it. It was a sort of diary in which the girl scribbled sentimental, trivial observations about her life and the people around her. Jamie read it and called me.

"Look what I've found," he said. "It's a diary."

I was upset and I knew he had a grudge against them, so I told him:

"Look, you have no business poking your nose into these things. Put it back."

"No, *compañero*," he insisted, "read it first and then we'll talk."

So I read it. In the most recent entry she wrote that things weren't going well, now it's a whole year, a whole year of my life wasted. She concluded that at any moment some problem arose she would abandon the house and leave without worrying about what happened to the others. I felt that she was even ready to blow the whole project as long as the two of them got out first.

At that time Antonio was living in the safe-house permanently and no longer had contact with the liaison member of the National Directorate. It was the Goth with his freedom of movement who maintained contact between the operational base and the organization. But now, sensing that an emergency was imminent, Antonio decided to take matters in his own hands:

I decided it was necessary to pull the diggers out, because in the safe-house we were facing a constant series of provocations. I left and renewed contact with the *compañero* of the National Directorate.

He was annoyed to see that we didn't have the capability or the resolution to overcome what seemed to be simple domestic problems. But they weren't simple domestic problems; there were so many of them that the quantity had transformed into quality. I explained the entire situation and told him that I really believed the Goth had gone crazy. I also told him about the girl's diary. I said: "There we are with the idea that at any moment the whole project could fall apart and that we're slaving away for nothing. All that enthusiasm, all that mystique and determination could simply evaporate, and you people have to take that into account."

"But what alternative do you propose?" he asked me.

And I really couldn't think of any alternative, because it was impossible by now to buy another lot and start building another house.

Nestor, a big bear of a man with years of experience in the labor union struggles of Peru, recalls this war of nerves with stoic resignation:

We wanted to keep on working with the couple — he tells us — but a moment arrived when they assumed an arrogant attitude and even tried blackmailing the organization, taking the position that we had to act in accordance with their needs and that they were going to dispose of their time in accordance with their personal problems. We had to keep on babysitting them until they finally went too far and simply abandoned the house. The house was in their name, they had bought it, and now they moved out. They deserted.

When the couple disappeared from the safe-house and didn't return that evening, Antonio ordered the diggers to lower all incriminating evidence into the tunnel shaft and to conceal the entrance with its sliding concrete cover. When that was accomplished, they locked the door to the "closet" and slipped out of the house in the darkness. Such was their frame of mind that they were prepared to believe the Goth had turned them in to the police and a raid might occur at any moment.

The couple dropped out of sight; the Goth did not appear for his scheduled meeting with the Directorate liaison, nor did he appear at any of the "automatic" backup meetings that are standard emergency measures in case someone misses a scheduled meeting. The organization wasted no time in tracing him down and sent a friend of his who had a strong influence over him to persuade him to attend an emergency meeting with Nestor and Antonio. The meeting took place in a restaurant in Lima. Antonio describes what took place:

The *compañero* (Nestor) accused him of deserting and reminded him that the MRTA was a politico-military organization that didn't tolerate such acts.

"I don't give a damn," the Goth told him.

"If you don't behave correctly, we will have to take other, stronger measures with you," the other warned.

"I've made a decision," the Goth said, "and if anything happens to me, there are people who are prepared to do something about it."

There it was at last, out in the open. The Goth had known all along that he was a key figure in the project and that his knowledge of the tunnel secret gave him a powerful hold over the organization. From the very outset he had used this leverage to do as he pleased, flouting party discipline, and now he was resorting to barefaced blackmail, confident that he held all the high cards. Nestor describes the showdown in this way:

We had a meeting to deal with the entire problem of the couple. The Goth took an intransigent attitude and said that if anything happened to him, he had left a letter with somebody denouncing the project we were carrying out.

Revolutionary organizations do not take kindly to betrayal or blackmail, and there was at least one instance in which the MRTA had "drastically sanctioned" a member who turned police informer and was responsible for the deaths and arrests of a number of militants. In the present case, however, there was no question of making a grim example of the Goth and his girlfriend: the stakes were simply too high and the consequences self-evident. Even if he was bluffing and the blackmail letter did not really exist, the disappearance of the couple would inevitably result in a police search of his home, discovery of the tunnel shaft and the end of all hope of liberating the four dozen MRTA militants incarcerated in Canto Grande. It was, in popular parlance, a mafia standoff. We return to Antonio's description of the outcome of the meeting:

The *companero* remained calm and said:
"Look, that doesn't bother us. Naturally, we want you to carry out your job. But you must understand one thing clearly: this project must not be betrayed."
And he went on stressing the political importance of the task and the justice of liberating the MRTA prisoners.
In the end, it was the Goth himself, in his frantic anxiety to get away from the safe-house, who offered a solution to the impasse.
"I have taken my measures," he repeated, "and I refuse to go back and live in that house, but I have a solution for you: bring in another couple, and I'll introduce them to the neighbors as relatives of mine."

It was the ideal solution to an extremely prickly security crisis. The safe-house had been vacated, and once again all work on the Canto Grande project came to a halt while the MRTA searched through its ranks for two tried and true militants who would unflinchingly assume the risks and the burden of providing caretaker cover for the tunnel diggers.

CHAPTER 7

From her early years, Paloma felt a patriotic urge to serve her country, and particularly the least privileged classes. She was an honors student in school and worked long hours in her free time with a Catholic youth organization engaged in charitable activities. She decided to become a medical doctor and won a scholarship to study medicine, specializing in rural medicine. She began collaborating with the MRTA in 1984 when her work with poor families in the interior of the country brought her to realize that a profound change in the social and economic structure of Peru was urgently needed before it could catch up with the developed world in health, education, social welfare and income distribution.

In 1988 she joined the MRTA as a full-time militant, and shortly thereafter she was asked to undertake a delicate mission of uncertain duration, which called for the utmost discretion and unswerving acceptance of party discipline. She accepted and was introduced to her presumptive husband, Luis Angel, with whom she was to live for the next 21 months. With scarcely a pause to catch her breath, she found herself in the operational safe-house of the Canto Grande tunnel project, while the Goth introduced Luis Angel to the neighbors as his uncle who was moving in with his wife to take care of the house during his absence. The Goth had promised the organization he would remain with the new couple for a week in order to help them familiarize themselves with the neighborhood, but after three days of introductions he left them to shift for themselves and never returned.

His departure afforded the organization an opportunity to retire the ancient Dodge taxi and purchase a Ford pickup truck with a greater capacity for hauling dirt. Luis Angel posed as a light cargo hauler who presumably spent his days making deliveries for customers at the Central Market in Lima. The only problem with that story was that Luis Angel did not know how to drive and did not possess a driver's license. He spent the first few weeks of his new career mastering the principles of driving and applying for a driver's license.

On the first day of our arrival — Paloma recalls — we went out to introduce ourselves to the neighbors, letting them know we were married and settling into the house and asking their advice about the water supply and where to shop. There was no running water in the area, and every three days or so we had to buy a truckload. This threatened to become a security problem as more and more diggers moved into the house. As for electricity, there were power lines on the street but we had no meter, so we had to buy our electricity from Señor Aldana, who in turn stole it from the power line running to Canto Grande. He didn't know and didn't care how much electricity we were using and always charged us the same price since he was getting it free.

Luis Angel's cartage work provided cover for him to bring construction materials to the house and to unload them in the patio. The neighbors never noticed that these materials disappeared underground instead of being reloaded into the truck.

By this time, the four diggers had moved back into the safe-house, and for the first time the work was going smoothly. Armando, because of his other duties, could only appear at the site at widely spaced intervals, and soon found that he was obliged to develop diplomatic skills as well as exercise his tunneling expertise.

Uncle Felix had long experience in construction work — Armando told us — and he was a proud and touchy man. I praised his idea of stuccoing the overhead of the tunnel, but I had to go slow about introducing the technique of timbering the tunnel. This had been used for centuries in Peruvian mines, but the old man had never worked in mines. I explained how it was done and how it protected against cave ins. In the end, Uncle Felix was convinced that he had thought of the technique himself.

Both Paloma and Luis Angel had authentic identity documents but, fortunately, were never called on to display them. The Canto Grande authorities had apparently lost interest in the neighborhood after their first security sweep.

Paloma's duties included cooking, housecleaning, health care, administration and logistics and, above all, security. Since Luis Angel was away all morning and all afternoon on his trucking business (in reality, purchasing construction materials for the tunnel as well as groceries and household supplies), she was the only one who could appear outside the house to keep an eye on the neighbors, consolidate her friendship with them and satisfy their curiosity.

Their closest neighbor, Señor Aldana, was proprietor of the sandpit behind the safe-house in a shady partnership with several of the Canto Grande prison officials. It is probable that Paloma's special efforts to cultivate his friendship and confidence led him to vouch for the couple with Canto Grande authorities.

She convinced him that they were a couple with limited means who were forging ahead economically because of Luis Angel's hard work. She herself supposedly took care of the bookkeeping end of the family business, billing customers and making sure that payments came in promptly.

Paloma's workday began early, inasmuch as she had to serve breakfast at 0630 so the diggers could set to work promptly at 0700. She had lunch ready by noon and dinner was served at 1900 after the diggers had knocked off, showered and had an hour to relax, listen to the radio or read.

When neighbors came calling, as occasionally happened, Paloma received them in the spacious living-dining room. The diggers washed their own plates and utensils, but Paloma had to see to it that the extra dishes were tucked out of sight and tried to keep nosy outsiders from wandering into the kitchen while meals for six hungry people were being prepared. When this did happen on one occasion, she had an explanation ready: she was preparing lunch for her husband and his working companions at the market.

The departure of the first couple enabled them to keep the back bedroom locked with the explanation that the Goth's personal belongings were stored there awaiting his return. In reality, besides concealing the tunnel entrance, the room served as dormitory for the diggers during the night and as storage area for the sacks of dirt during the day.

"Didn't any of the neighbors ever see or hear any of the diggers?" we asked Paloma.

No, — she replied — the boys who did the excavating led as confined an existence as did the *compañeros* in Canto Grande whom they were trying to free, because they were shut up for two months at a time, never showing their noses outside the house. Then they'd be given a week off to get away, unwind and lead a normal life for a few days. As for the noise, I kept the radio going all day long and until well after dinner. Once when I was visiting one of the neighbors, she told me: "You really love music, don't you?"

"Oh, yes," I told her, "music is my lifeblood. Cooped up in this empty house all day long, I'd feel like a ghost if it weren't for the radio."

Besides that, we soon had eight big, noisy dogs, as well as chickens and ducks, and I'd talk to them when I was sweeping or watering the plants and vegetables. The strange thing was that the dogs accepted the diggers in the house and the neighbors when they came calling, but they hated the *Republicano* guards and would set up a terrible commotion whenever they came by. They were a fantastic security factor for us.

The neighbors never suspected any unusual activities going on in the safe-house. Paloma and her "husband" regularly attended festivities such as birthday parties, appeared at wakes when someone died, and Paloma visited the sick, bringing them delicacies and suggesting remedies, although she never let it be known that she was a physician.

Inasmuch as many of the neighbors worked in a civilian capacity within Canto Grande itself, Paloma was able to glean much useful intelligence concerning conditions inside the prison, such as when a group of *Republicanos* was to be transferred and who was to replace them, when a general cell search was about to take place, what was the military background and personal character of the new commandant who had just taken over.

Meanwhile, for the first time, work on the tunnel was advancing smoothly though painfully. The first leg now extended under the street fronting the house and well into the walled off vacant lots, and Paloma would occasionally stroll through the lots to determine whether or not she could hear digging noises underfoot. Since she couldn't, the diggers abandoned their pointed wooden stakes and started using what was to be their principal digging tool: the crowbar. Paloma reported that she couldn't hear metal clanging against rock either. The tunnel was now approximately eight meters below ground and advancing horizontally.

As the tunnel grew longer, digging conditions steadily grew worse. Heat at the tunnel face became oppressive and the air grew thicker. The diggers worked in briefs and tennis shoes, carried bottled water and soft drinks with them to prevent dehydration and kept an oxygen bottle resuscitator at hand in case one of them fainted from lack of oxygen. They alleviated their working conditions by splashing the tunnel face with waste water from their underground shower to cool the air and settle the dust.

Large rocks were the chief problem in the first, 35-meter leg of the tunnel, according to Jaime. The team christened this section "Che Vive" (Che lives) in commemoration of Che Guevara, who had died 20 years earlier in the jungles of Bolivia. With four diggers at work, the tunnel advanced at the rate of 1 1/2 to 2 meters a week. One man hacked at the tunnel face with a crowbar, another filled jute sacks with the dirt while a third hauled the sacks back to the tunnel entrance. The fourth would busy himself timbering the shaft every two meters and stuccoing the exposed overhead with a cement and water mixture. In the early stages, the diggers exchanged jobs every several hours to keep boredom from setting in, but as the air grew fouler at the tunnel face the digger became exhausted after 30 minutes and had to be relieved by the sack-loader, who in turn was relieved by the transporter after a half-hour's exertion.

The "Che Vive" leg of the tunnel was finished on October 23, 1988. Jaime remembers the date vividly because it was his birthday. The team celebrated its completion at dinner with a bottle of wine. Armando, who joined in the celebration, calculated that the first sector had taken them clear of Aldana's sandpit, and they could now safely make a sharp left turn and head directly for guard tower No. 8 which marked the entrance to Canto Grande. The direction, which he had calculate with a surveyor's theodolite, was to be South 34 degrees Celsius.

Surveyors have an immense advantage over clandestine tunnelers in that they can measure precise distances above ground and determine exact angles as needed. One of the chief errors in calculating the length of time that would be required to excavate the Canto Grande tunnel was that they estimated the distance from the safe-house to guard tower no. 8 as a bit more than 100 meters. To make a more accurate calculation, Armando and Uncle Felix had to chip out a peephole in the patio wall facing the prison, use the theodolite telescope to count the number of bricks rising vertically from the ground to the top of the outer prison wall, estimate the thickness of the mortar between each brick and then multiply the known thickness of each brick plus the mortar by the number of brick layers to arrive at the estimated height of the wall. Then by measuring the exact angle from the ground to the top of the wall, they were able to calculate that the distance from the safe-house to the prison wall was nearly 200 meters. This meant extra months of digging.

As the tunnel took a sharp turn and started extending in the new direction, the air at the tunnel face became virtually unbreathable. The diggers suffered headaches, respiratory infections and fainting spells and grew exhausted more quickly. Armando, foreseeing this problem, had designed an air extractor system, using an exhaust fan set up in the first vertical tunnel entrance which was no longer used and plastic tubing strung along one side of the overhead to within a short distance of the tunnel face. The fan sucked dead air out of the excavation area, and new, cooler air flowed in to replace it. This, plus the water splashed on the digging area, enabled the diggers to abandon their filter masks and for the first time to breathe freely as they worked. A plumbing system was also installed to bring running water along the length of the excavation, and the primitive system of carrying waste water from the shower could be eliminated.

As the tunnel grew longer, it also took more time to drag the sacks full of dirt from the working area back to the tunnel entrance, and this became the next bottleneck that had to be resolved.

Armando had foreseen this development as well and had decided it was impractical to lay rails along the floor and use traditional mine cars to haul away the dirt. Instead, the team member in charge of timbering and stuccoing was given the additional task of smoothing and cementing the tunnel floor so a small, rubber-tired vehicle could trundle over it. Several types and sizes of carts were experimented with before the diggers hit upon the optimum combination: a wagon with high sides that could transport between six and eight sacks of dirt in one trip.

These technical advances made it feasible to bring in two more diggers who joined the team in December 1988. The tunnel advanced more rapidly on the straightaway towards tower no. 8, which was christened "*La lucha continúa*" (The struggle continues.)

When she wasn't otherwise occupied with household duties, Paloma would descend the vertical shaft into the tunnel entrance to tie the mouths of the filled sacks so they could be hoisted to the storage room for later transfer to the Ford pickup. In the early days, the sacks had to be hauled up the 4 1/2 meter shaft by brute force, but later a collapsible tripod with a pulley was installed to make the lifting easier. Several members of the team awoke with Luis Angel at 4 a.m. to remove the filled sacks from the storage room and load them into the truck. Luis Angel, who now had a legal driver's license after months of bureaucratic delay, left in the truck before dawn, carted the dirt to a fill in an entirely different area of the Lima suburbs and emptied it, sack by sack, there. He would then do the necessary purchasing together with Antonio who was now working away from the safe-house as full-time project coordinator and liaison with the MRTA leadership. When Luis Angel returned home for lunch, the pickup would be loaded with sacks of dirt once again, to be dumped during the afternoon. The Ford broke down frequently and sacks of dirt piled up in the storage space while it was being repaired. For another thing, Luis Angel had learned to drive, but nobody had ever bothered to tell him that the oil has to be added and changed at frequent intervals if an automobile is to continue performing faithfully. This oversight, plus the fact that there was more dirt coming out of the tunnel than the medium-sized pickup could carry away, was eventually to result in the retirement of the Ford and its replacement with a more capacious Dodge pickup that functioned faithfully to the very end.

CHAPTER 8

Rodrigo was the first member of the MRTA's National Directorate to fall into the hands of the police. Although he was clandestine, he occasionally had to confer with members of other Peruvian organizations that were legal, and on one of these occasions an informer told the police where they could find him. The police followed him when he left the meeting and arrested him on the street. He was taken to DIRCOTE where he was systematically tortured for five days, undergoing the classic repertoire of police torturers all over Latin America. The "softening up" process consisted of beating and kicking, arm-twisting, hanging him for hours by his wrists and heels, after which came the "serious" work with the electric *picana*, or cattle prod, and finally the *tina* or bathtub. This is known in other Latin American countries as the "submarine." The prisoner is hand- and leg-cuffed and forced to kneel beside a bathtub. His head is shoved under water — which is frequently filled with human feces and urine — and held there until his lungs nearly burst. Rodrigo has this to say about his experience:

The bathtub is the worst form of torture. Physical pain, however great, can be endured, because the only thing necessary is to withstand the pain. It's not easy, but possible. Drowning, though, produces terrible psychological effects. The efficient torturer not only produces pain but the sensation of abandonment, uncertainty, anguish and desperation, and drowning achieves all of that. When you start threshing uncontrollably, they lift your head out of the water and then push you under again. This goes on for hours.

After five days, Rodrigo still hadn't talked, and he was too well-known a political figure to be tortured to death, so DIRCOTE sent him to the Ministry of Justice for trial and sentencing. On 27 August 1987, he was remanded to Canto Grande.

That opened a new phase of my life, a new experience — Rodrigo tells us. — When I arrived, the first thing that surprised me was a certain freedom of movement. I thought it would be a much more closed system with greater physical control and all prisoners locked in their cells. But instead I saw that all the *compañeros* were free to move about inside the pavilion. They had an entire floor to themselves and they had installed a library and had storage space for their personal belongings. They could go down to the ground floor and organize sports in the patio. They even had the MRTA symbols painted on the walls. So they could actually lead their own way of life. I was the first member of the Directorate to fall prisoner, and my arrival marked a turn in the political life of the group. It gave us an opportunity to concentrate on ideological formation of the group, the chance to organize schools and lectures. With my arrival there were 28 MRTA prisoners in Canto Grande. They were already organized into a detachment of three squads, each squad consisting of nine men. There were leaders at the head of each squad, and the four of us made up the internal Directorate of the party in the pavilion.

Rodrigo learned from the others that the relaxation of security restrictions had not been a free gift by any means. The prisoners had won each slender privilege by fighting for their rights through hunger strikes and public pressure brought to bear on the prison administration by their families and other organizations through the Peruvian press and radio.

Another factor in the gradual relaxation was the administrative chaos prevailing in the INPE, or National Penitentiary Institute, which was responsible for prison administration. Peru was undergoing a severe economic crisis, and the national budget had been pared to the bone. The food budget for each prisoner in Peru was whittled to an absurd half dollar per day. Corrupt administrators in INPE headquarters siphoned off cash from that amount, and the prison commandant also took his cut. Then supply officials within the prison took home five kilos of rice out of every 100 kilos that arrived and five bags of beans out of 50. The prisoners themselves wound up with approximately 25 cents worth of food each. The deterioration in the quantity and quality of food led to prison riots and strikes by both the political and common prisoners. Prison authorities were unable to improve the prison diet and unwilling to put an end to the corruption, so they had to offer concessions which cost them nothing. An extra visiting day was added on Wednesdays. Instead of restricting compassionate visits to the *venusterio* (literally "Venus' quarters") they were permitted within the cell blocks, with one cell blanketed off to permit privacy.

When the prison was first opened, visitors could bring nothing in with them — Rodrigo describes another forced concession — because in the beginning the penitentiary provided everything. But soon the authorities gave the prisoners less and began to permit the entry of fruits and a few other things. As the budget grew smaller they permitted the entry of rice and beans. INPE's strategy was to force the prisoners to pay for their own survival. Thus, all sorts of things including jam and canned fruits were permitted inside, and a few enterprising prisoners even set up their own retail stores inside the prison.

This change in the regulations led to still another problem for the enforcement of prison security: when family visitors were forbidden to bring anything with them into Canto Grande, body searches were rapid and easy to control. But when families started bringing in baskets of groceries, inspection of the contents became a tedious, time-consuming affair and, inevitably, the guards grew lax and allowed more dubious items to enter. For example, MRTA propaganda and all sorts of "subversive" literature were waved through with no more than a cursory glance.

The health situation of the prisoners was equally bad — Rodrigo continues. — There was no medical attention to speak of. Prisoners who got knifed or beaten up in fights received first aid at the prison clinic by the nurses on duty, but prisoners had to buy their own medicines. We of the MRTA had to install our own health clinic, and we even brought in orthodontic dental equipment. A dentist friend would visit us on Sundays to fix our teeth.

In this environment, the lowest level prison guards became corrupt, and a prisoner who wished to visit a friend in another pavilion had only to fork over a quarter or a candy bar to obtain permission to do so.

There was a national scandal connected with the construction of Canto Grande itself — Rodrigo told us. — The Ubarde Company, a Spanish concern, won the construction contract and employed all the traditional tools of graft: kickbacks, over-invoicing, shoddy materials and failure to install systems agreed to in the contract. The closed-circuit television system was never installed, for example, and neither were the underground electronic sensors to detect digging noises. All of these breakdowns and failures, of course, benefited us.

One of the group activities of the MRTA prisoners was the maintenance of a wall newspaper on the ground floor of Pavilion 2A. Its contents were changed twice weekly, on Wednesdays and Saturdays. It was called *La Columna* because it was mounted on one of the concrete columns that supported the building. The name also evoked the guerrilla columns that were fighting in the Andes and, of course, the idea of a newspaper column. Originally, the mural newspaper had been intended for the edification of family members who came to visit, but as time went on its purpose subtly changed.

Every morning at 0800 and every evening at 1700 all prisoners had to assemble on the ground floor of the pavilion for roll call. A detachment of approximately 15 *Republicanos* would enter the pavilion while this was taking place, and invariably, five or six of the guards would crowd around the *La Columna* display and read its contents. This spontaneous interest led the political prisoners to realize that they could use *La Columna* as a means of subliminal communication with the guards: an implement of psychological warfare to present the MRTA viewpoint sympathetically and to gradually politicize the prison personnel.

This was part of a grander design to establish friendly relations with the *Republicanos* and lull them into believing that the MRTA members were resigned to their fate and only interested in improving their living conditions within Canto Grande and leading a tranquil life until they were released. This attitude was in marked contrast to the tactics of the *Senderistas* in the prison who constantly provoked and defied their captors as an integral part of their own ideological vision of the world. The program went to such length that in the end MRTA basketball and football teams were staging tournaments with their *Republicano* challengers, and the standing joke was that if the MRTA team won they would walk out of the prison and leave the guards locked up.

This cultivation of friendly relations with the guards led directly to another incredible absurdity: the incident of the pavilion padlock.

When Canto Grande was opened, each pavilion gate was secured by a built-in electronic lock that could be opened or closed by remote control from the central rotunda. As previously explained, the common and political prisoners soon disabled these locks by jamming them with small wires and metal scrap. The prison administration had no funds to repair or replace this expensive lockup system, so it was replaced with a simple system of padlocks and chains. The pavilion guard held the key, and when a prisoner had to visit the health clinic, the guard would unlock the pavilion gate, lock it behind him and accompany the prisoner to the clinic, reversing the process on the return journey.

One visiting day, the padlock to Pavilion 2A suffered the same fate as the previous locks had. One of the MRTA prisoners had stuffed the keyhole with wire, and when the pavilion guard tried to open it, the key jammed and broke off in the lock. In the mounting clamor of family members to enter the pavilion, the guard obtained an iron rod and used it as a lever to break off the hasp. As luck would have it, there was no spare padlock in the prison storeroom to replace it and no way of securing the gate when lockup time came around. The gate remained unsecured that night, guarded against delinquent intruders from other pavilions by MRTA sentinels armed with *chavetas*, wicked long knives. By morning, however, it was locked again. One of the MRTA prisoners had offered the use of a sturdy padlock which he used to secure his chest of personal belongings.

Next morning when the guard detachment showed up for the 0800 roll-call, an MRTA delegate opened the gate and let them in. As they prepared to leave the sergeant in charge asked for the key.

"Give you the key?" Rodrigo said indignantly, "This is our lock and our key. Go get your own."

His logic was impeccable, and amazingly enough, this stratagem worked, simply because the prison authorities had no budget authority to buy padlocks and chains. For the next two years the prison guards had to request permission of the MRTA whenever they had to enter the Pavilion 2A redoubt. MRTA sentinels stood guard at the gate around the clock, and they always unlocked the gate for the prison guards, though they sometimes delayed things for a few minutes to give their *compañeros* upstairs time to burn any incriminating messages from the outside.

Little by little — Rodrigo comments — the *Republicanos* lost control over the individual pavilions so that in the end they could only exercise their authority over the central patio around the Rotunda and the area between the Admissions building and the outer wall of the prison. Essentially, their security function was reduced to preventing prisoners from strolling out the main gate. Inside the pavilions an anarchic free will prevailed, and the prisoners in each block generated their own style of life and organization. The *Senderistas* and MRTA pavilions were controlled by their party organizations, while the pavilions of the common prisoners were run by Mafia-type *capos* who imposed their will through squads of strong-arm thugs who were the most hardened criminals, or by imprisoned drug traffickers who controlled their junkie underlings by doling out drugs.

Besides establishing amicable relations with the prison guards, the MRTA had to learn how to relate to the common prisoners.

We found we had a lot to learn — Rodrigo recalls ruefully — because we were political prisoners, and the political is ingenuous in establishing a relationship with those people. They had a word to define themselves: they said, "we rats." Rats in the sense that they have a very corrupt, rotten mentality. They are always seeking the worst side of things and always looking for the second, third and fourth intention of your every gesture. If you greet them, it's difficult to go on from there...and if you don't say "Hello," they say, "Why are you turning your back on me?" In addition, they never trust anybody, because they know that their best friend today can stab them in the back tomorrow. That's how things are on the *lumpen* level; their system of values is completely destroyed. They seek only benefits that are absolutely selfish; they try only to turn every situation to their personal advantage, and they're suspicious of everybody cloe.

The MRTA learned the hard way that it was useless to try friendly persuasion in dealing with the organized gangs of common prisoners; the one thing they understood and respected was brute force, and they used it against the MRTA in early 1988 to evict them from Pavilion 3A where they were first quartered.

"What was the reason for this attack?" we asked Rodrigo, and he replied with a colorful analogy:

"It was basically a matter of overcrowding, because there was only so much space in the prison, and the authorities kept stuffing in more prisoners. Let's say you're standing on a small platform, and somebody steps up beside you and jostles you every time he moves. Then a third climbs up on the platform and starts stepping on your toes while a fourth tries to get up there as well. This is more or less what happened in each pavilion. For example, the prison only had running water for a half hour each day, and during that half hour we had to collect water for the whole day, besides bathing and washing our clothing. This created constant quarreling. Apart from this, there was a precedent that caused the common prisoners to distrust the political prisoners. Way back in '82 or '83, even before the MRTA appeared on the scene, the prisoners of *Sendero Luminosa* were mingled with common prisoners throughout Peru, and the overcrowding of prisons had already started. Early one morning while the common prisoners were still asleep, *Senderista* contingents armed with sticks and knives forcibly evicted them from the cell blocks they claimed as their own and from then on defended their stronghold by force. In Canto Grande the common prisoners saw that we were increasing in numbers and in strength, and in the prison there exists a functional logic of "getting the jump" on the other. If you see that your enemy is going to kill you, you get the jump on him and kill him first. They reasoned that we were eventually going to evict them, so they decided to evict us first. So one day they caught us completely off guard and threw us out of Pavilion 3-A. We learned many things from that. In the first place that in prison we had to arm ourselves with knives, lances, shoemaker's awls and leather-cutting knives, Bowie knives...all these things simply for self-defense. We had to organize ourselves militarily, establish an intelligence service to learn what the other prisoners were thinking. We had to maintain our own unity and follow a policy of alliances with certain sectors in order to neutralize the rest. In short we had to undergo an intensive education. A few months went by and one day we fell upon the leaders of the gang that controlled the drug traffic in the prison. We rounded up the *capos*, gave them a good threshing, broke their heads and threw them out. That was when we installed ourselves on the fourth floor of Pavilion 2-A. That changed their notions about us. They saw that we could take care of ourselves on the battlefield, and from then on — this happened in mid-1988 — we enjoyed a more normal and tranquil environment. We did make some efforts to rescue some of the common prisoners who seemed less hardened than the others, but with no positive results. What you can do is neutralize them and keep them from attacking you, but to change them, offer them a new value system, is impossible.

After Rodrigo arrived and took charge of the MRTA contingent, a new esprit de corps imbued the group. None of the prisoners knew about the tunnel plan other than Rodrigo and his three lieutenants, but the rest were assigned new tasks, principal of which was to carefully map the interior of the prison and to explore the subterranean corridors and sewage ducts until they could make their way through them in pitch darkness, opening barred gates as necessary. The inside coordination of the escape plan was starting to take form.

Mapping Canto Grande from the inside was almost as slow a process as digging the tunnel from the outside. The work had to be done in the dead of night or in the early morning hours, but little by little the MRTA teams engaged in the exploration were able to gain access to nearly all the subterranean tunnels and the sewage system that ringed the central patio of the prison. They obtained or made duplicate keys to barred doors and even obtained access to Canto Grande's electrical switchboards, which were located underground. Were the need to arise, they were capable of cutting off electricity to all the pavilions and the internal spotlights that illuminated the central patio and rotunda.

Another strategic requirement was to gain control of the ground floor of the pavilion, which gave access to the 2A patio where it was expected that the tunnel would surface. Each cell block in a pavilion contains 8 cells, and each cell accommodates 4 prisoners, or a total of 32 on each of the three habitable floors. The ground floor of each pavilion is a roofed open space except for the concrete columns that support the entire edifice. In the original plans, this space was reserved for a mess hall and prisoners workshops as well as latrines and showers. As the MRTA population grew beyond the 32-man capacity of the fourth floor and reached a total of 39 they received permission from the prison authorities to wall off a space of 10 by 20 meters in one corner of the open area and furnish it with bunks, tables and benches. This became the living quarters for between 15 and 20 MRTA prisoners and gave them the capability of controlling by force, if need be, the ground floor of the pavilion and the outdoor patio as well.

The idea of expanding their living quarters to the ground floor seemed necessary and logical to the MRTA contingent, and they fell to work with a will to accomplish it. But, we asked, what about the other strange activities they had to carry out, such as mapping the interior of the prison virtually inch by inch? Didn't some of the prisoners who were ignorant of the tunnel project, suspect some special plan was afoot?

In the very final stages — Rodrigo explained — we had to bring a few others in on the plan, because we needed them to accomplish special tasks. And, of course you're right; a prisoner's mind works overtime with thoughts of escape, and many of the others — perhaps most of them — smelled that something was up, and that probably another tunnel was underway. However, none of them suspected that it was being dug from the outside into the prison itself.

But one of the things you learn in clandestine existence is to not ask questions. The *compañeros* all had confidence in the Directorate and knew that in good time they would learn what was going on. They knew they were free to discuss political lines and tactics freely and to argue and disagree all they wanted until a decision was reached. But strategic, compartmented tasks are another matter entirely, and there absolute discipline, discretion, secrecy and unswerving trust in the leadership is required. They all understood and accepted that, and they all carried out whatever tasks were demanded of them, no matter how strange they may have seemed.

Now two teams were working on the Canto Grande escape project. The team inside had been forged by Rodrigo and his lieutenants into three squads as disciplined and motivated as the outside team of diggers, but also as blinded to the ultimate objective of their efforts as were the men in the tunnel when, as occasionally happened, somebody accidentally pulled out a plug in the lighting system.

THE TIME TUNNEL-III

Túpac Amaru's rebellion did not end with the death of its leader and his family, but continued flaring up in different Andean regions for the next several years: an indigenous precursor of the Latin American independence movement that finally freed the continent from the Spanish crown in the early 1820s.

Peruvian independence brought the *criollo* descendants of the Spanish *conquistadores* to power but achieved little or no change or betterment for the mass of Indians, mestizos, mulattos and Asian immigrants who made up the bulk of the Peruvian population. It was a racist, caste-ridden society, governed by a white-skinned, aristocratic elite whose principal concern was to maintain the status quo that worked to its exclusive benefit.

The extensive latifundios in the Andean highlands were administered in feudal style by the owners themselves or by the *gamonales,* cruel overseers who were given a free hand in exploiting the Indian peoples under their dominion as more and more *latifundistas* absented themselves from their holdings to build stately mansions for themselves in Lima. From 1821 until the end of the century, the central government was in the hands of military *caudillos* who fomented ethnic disputes between the *quechua* and *aymara* peoples to maintain a divided Indian population.

In the latter part of the 19th century and the early 20th century, the "Aristocratic Republic" of Peru was shaken by eruptions of seething discontent triggered by such disparate events as imposition of a salt tax, the appearance of the self-styled "Virgin of Rosario," and sporadic reappearances of the "millenialist" doctrine, which called for a generalized war against the whites and expropriation of their lands to restore the ancient Inca empire and communal ownership of property. The last "millenialist" uprisings against the white overlords were stamped out in 1915 and 1921.

CHAPTER 9

An MRTA courier arrived in Lima on February 2, 1989 to inform "Comandante Rolando" that his presence was urgently required the following day at a secret meeting of the Regional Directorate of the Central Front in Guancayo, Peru. Several guerrilla columns of the MRTA were operating on the Central Front, a strategic area both politically and militarily. The *Sendero Luminoso* was also active there, and the government had declared a state of emergency in the zone. The only feasible transport link was a bus leaving Lima at 2200 hours for Guancayo.

Rolando's regular armed escort had been dispatched on another mission, since he had not anticipated that he would be traveling. A substitute traveling companion had to be found immediately, and time was of the essence inasmuch as he did not receive the message until mid-afternoon. A young girl who was an MRTA collaborator, not a full-fledged militant, was hastily selected and told to pack for the trip. She was inexperienced, but her principal role was simply to provide cover for Rolando — they were to travel as man and wife — and he foresaw no difficulties during the uncomfortable all-night journey.

The couple arrived on schedule at 1000 hours the following morning and registered at a tourist hotel in the center of town. Rolando, who had gotten no sleep during the trip, though his companion dozed fitfully, stretched out on the bed and fell asleep, while the girl went out to make contact with the MRTA leaders in Guancayo.

She returned to the hotel at 1500 hours to find the area and the hotel itself swarming with police and soldiers. As fate would have it, the Peruvian Prime Minister, Armando Villanueva del Campo, and his Minister of Defense had arrived for a surprise visit to the troubled Guancayo area and had taken quarters in the hotel. Uncertain and nervous, the girl entered the lobby to try to telephone a warning to Rolando. She was stopped and her handbag was searched. Inside it, the police found a pistol and a hand grenade. She was whisked away to an unoccupied room, slapped around by her interrogators, and she broke easily, confessing that her companion was occupying a room in the hotel.

Minutes later, using the hotel's master key, a group of hooded soldiers armed with automatic combat rifles, broke into Rolando's room and placed him under arrest. He too was armed with a pistol and a grenade but had no chance to use them. His captors handcuffed and hooded him, took him downstairs and placed him in an automobile of the Peruvian Investigative Police (PIP). A jurisdictional dispute immediately broke out between the members of the PIP and the army officers who had arrested him and claimed the right to take him into custody. Finally, the investigative police agreed to follow an army vehicle to the Guancayo fortress and turn their prisoner over to the military authorities, but as soon as the other car turned into the fortress gates, the automobile bearing Rolando zipped off down the street and delivered him to the local headquarters of the PIP.

The PIP now had in custody a well-dressed couple, both of whom had been relieved of pistols and grenades and who bore identity documents that were undoubtedly false. They did not know who Rolando was, but they were certain they had landed a big fish. Both Rolando and the girl, who was by now overwhelmed by the enormity of her multiple errors, refused to cooperate with their interrogators, so the police faxed a blowup of Rolando's fingerprints to their headquarters in Lima and settled down to wait. Within hours the answer came back: the nameless man, "Comandante Rolando" to his comrades in arms, was no other than Victor Polay Campo, top leader of the MRTA and a big fish indeed.

Who was this Victor Polay Campo? Among other things, he was the man upon whose head Peruvian President Alan Garcia had placed a $25,000 reward for any information leading to his capture, and this despite the fact the two of them were boyhood friends and former roommates during the period of their European exile.

Victor was born into an *Aprista* family in 1951. His father was one of the founders of the APRA movement and had spent 10 years in different Peruvian prisons for his political convictions. His mother was an equally dedicated member of the party, and as a boy Victor regularly attended APRA demonstrations and rallies with his parents. At the age of eight, despite his mother's admontions to stay out of politics, he joined the *Chicos Apristas Peruanos* (CHAP), which was a sort of a Cub Scout movement of the party and when he became a member of the Aprista Youth Movement (*Juventide Aprista Peruana*) and after that the Aprista University Commando (*Comando Universitario Aprista*). He also joined the Boy Scouts and became a student leader in high school. In the university, where he studied engineering, he was appointed to the APRA Conjunction Bureau (*Buro de Conjunciones*) — a testing ground for bright young *Apristas* who showed promise of developing into political leaders. There he worked alongside Alan Garcia, who was to become the first *Aprista* president of Peru between 1985 and 1990 when the MRTA was growing into a force to be reckoned with on the Peruvian political scene.

In 1970-71, Victor became secretary-general of the Aprista University Commando, a group of fiery student militants whose activities frequently overstepped the law. As a consequence of one of these episodes, he was arrested in 1972 and served a six-month sentence in Lurigancho prison. When released, the party sent him abroad to cool off. He went to Spain and registered at the Complutense University in El Escorial. Alan Garcia , also in exile, was a fellow student there, and the two of them shared an apartment. When funds ran short, both of them traveled to Geneva where they worked as ditch-diggers to earn money for further studies.

In late 1973, Victor moved to Paris and registered at Nanterres University to study sociology and economics. Over the previous years he had experienced increasing discrepancies with Victor Haya de la Torre's leadership of the APRA movement, and while in Paris, he joined a cell of the *Peruvian Movimiento Izquierdista Revolucionario* (MIR). Paris, during the 70's and 80's, played host to political exiles from all over Latin America, and Victor met and befriended many of them.

He returned to Peru in 1975 as an active member of MIR "*El Militante,*" one of the many factions into which the MIR was divided. During the next two years he traveled between Peru and Europe, carrying out various revolutionary tasks, and in 1977 he returned to Peru definitively.

But that was 12 action-filled years in the past, and now, hooded and handcuffed in the back seat of a police patrol car, Victor contemplated the ironic series of flukes that had brought about his downfall.

"It was my own fault of course," he admitted to us in a Lima safe-house. "I should never have traveled with some-one who was untrained to react flexibly to emergencies."

"But how senseless to try to call you from inside the hotel instead of going to another phone."

"Exactly," he shrugged. If I had been with my regular security escort, he would never have committed such a mistake. Most likely, he would have drawn his weapon and started firing to warn me. But sometimes you have only a few minutes to make a decision, and that's when mistakes occur, because you take it for granted that things will go smoothly."

"Looking back, it seems as though everything had been set up by fate. If we had traveled with my escort, it wouldn't have happened. If we had chosen another hotel, or if Villanueva had selected a different hotel, things wouldn't have turned out the way they did. But in any case it was my fault for having made a bad decision."

"How do you account for the rivalry between the PIP and the army?" we asked.

"It was the army that captured me. But it was PIP that had taken me into custody and done all the investigative work. It was primarily a case of institutional jealousy or beauracratic in fighting. However, the PIP officers also knew that if I had been turned over to the army zone commander, Gen. Delgado Rojas, he would have "disappeared" me. That man is a savage killer, as he proved during the Los Molinos wipeout a few months later."

Late that night, Victor was taken in a three car convoy as far as Moroy, a mining town in the Andes. Gen. Delgado Rojas expressed his outrage by harassing the convoy with army trucks and automobiles but stopped short of employing violence to halt it and recapture the prisoner. A snowstorm also slowed their progress. Finally, at 0400, another military convoy coming from Lima met the first group, and Victor was turned over to them. He arrived at the Lima Prefecture of Police in the early morning hours and, hooded and handcuffed, he was placed in a darkened maximum security cell where, for the next hours he had time to ponder the political consequences of his capture and the damage to the image of the MRTA when the arrest of its top leader was announced.

An eternity later, he was hauled rudely from his cell and marched down a corridor to another room where, for the first time, his hood was removed and he stood blinking in the sudden glare of light.

The first person I saw — he told us — was a tall, husky blonde type in front of me. I looked around and saw I was surrounded by blonde, Nordic people in uniform. The first thing that popped into my mind was that I had been turned over to the U.S. Embassy and had fallen into the hands of the CIA. But then, sitting in the back, I recognized the chiefs of the Investigative Police, the National Police, the Civil Guard and the Republican Guard. They were all staring at me as though I were a goldfish in a bowl, and I realized that the blonde types were officers of the Peruvian Navy, which is an aristocratic, racist organization that selects candidates from clean-cut Aryan stock.

The first voice I heard was that of the Prime Minister, Armando Villanueva del Campo. Villanueva is one of the APRA's historic leaders and was a candidate for the presidency of APRA in 1980. He walked into the room at that moment and said, "Hello, Victor, how are you?" That's the way he talks. There were other people with him from different political sectors.

"I'm glad to see you," he went on, "because as you know, I'm an old friend of your father's and we spent many years in prison together. He asked me to respect your situation and to treat you with consideration." He approached me and said: "Besides, we'd like to talk to you about what's happening in the country. We've been watching the things your people are doing, and we think it's time to engage in some dialogue about the situation."

"That's a decision of the enemy's that you've adopted," I told him. "Our objectives are not to engage in dialogue; our objectives are revolutionary. You are part of the government, a government that is massacring people and violating human rights, and under these conditions I don't see any possibilities of dialogue."

I had nothing else to say, so I kept quiet. Villanueva went over to talk to the generals, but then looked back and said: "Why is he handcuffed? Take off his handcuffs." A typical politician playing the generosity game.

They removed my handcuffs, and the whole confrontation lasted only a few minutes before they led me out. Of course they put the cuffs on me and hooded me again before they tossed me back in the cell, but I was relieved because I had been displayed publicly and couldn't be disappeared.

Victor was transferred to the cells of DIRCOTE and was subjected to the normal routine of psychological torture: he was kept awake, dragged from his cell at any hour of day or night for interrogation, threatened with death if he didn't talk, all to no avail.

The director of the Investigative Police came to see me — Victor told us — and he said: "Either you'll talk or we'll make you talk."

"You know I'm not going to talk," I answered. "You can cut off my hands and feet if you want to, but make no mistake; you'll also have to assume responsibility for the consequences. I'm speaking as the *comandante* of the MRTA."

He held up a hand and said: "Don't take things that way and don't worry, we're not going to torture you.

The psychological torture continued, particularly when he was hooded and could not identify his interrogator. When he was taken out of his cell and marched down a corridor. He heard an unusual bustle and the murmur of many voices, and he guessed what was about to happen: he was going to be displayed to the press as a trophy of the government's anti-terrorist program. His mind shifted into overdrive as he considered his alternatives. He had two precedents to guide his course of action. When Osmán Morote, second in command of the *Sendero Luminoso* was arrested, he was also brought before a press conference for questioning. Morote had been completely submissive and displayed a defeated air. He had taken the position that he was innocent, that he didn't belong to the *Sendero*, that he knew nothing about the charges against him and he was unwilling to answer questions from the press.

The other precedent had happened only the day before when he was being questioned by one of the Investigative Police. The man had told him he was a terrorist and he was going to die.

"Who's a terrorist?" Victor retorted. "You are talking to a revolutionary, a guerilla fighter."

"No," the policeman said. "Alan Garcia himself has said that you are an ordinary delinquent and are going to be tried as such."

Now Victor's hood was stripped off and he found himself in a crowded room, facing approximately 120 newspapermen. A police general stood up and started telling the throng about the circumstances of Victor's capture. Victor interrupted him by shouting that he was a revolutionary, a guerilla and a member of the MRTA, and he demanded that he be treated as a prisoner of war.

"Furthermore," he told the assembled newsmen, "I accuse Alan Garcia of being a delinquent himself, with no moral authority to accuse us of delinquency. It is he who has enriched himself at the expense of the people and the state..."

He was interrupted at this point and dragged out of the room, while the newsmen protested noisily that he should be allowed to speak. The chief of police followed Victor into the room where they had taken him and tried to reason with him.

"You're making us look ridiculous," he said. "You have to go back out there, and you can holler 'Long live Tupac

Amaru,' or 'Long live the MRTA ,' but don't start accusing Alan Garcia."

"I'll go back if you want me to, but I'm going to say the same thing, so you decide what's most convenient for you."

The general pondered that for a moment and then returned to the other room and announced that the press conference was suspended.

After the standard 15 days in DIRCOTE, Victor was taken before the judicial authorities and remanded to Canto Grande.

He arrived in a caravan of police cars with sirens wailing and was placed in solitary confinement in a cell so tiny he could neither stand up nor lie down. In one corner was a Turkish toilet clogged with feces that emitted a horrid stench. He had to sleep on the floor curled up in a ball. This treatment was a clear violation of the penal code, which prescribes solitary confinement for no more than 15 days for prisoners who have committed serious violations of the regulations, such as attempting to escape or killing or wounding another prisoner.

Victor was confined in this cell for six weeks, until word of his cruel and unusual punishment leaked out, and the MRTA and human rights organizations launched a national campaign on his behalf that resulted in the Minister of Justice and a judge visiting Canto Grande to see for themselves the inhumane conditions to which he was subjected. The Minister ordered him removed from the punishment cell and moved to the *venusterio*, an area that had previously accommodated intimate visits by prisoner's wives but was now used as the maximum security pavilion. He was given a decent room and a private bathroom, but he was still in solitary confinement; the only other occupant of the Venusterio's third floor was the *Senderista*, Morote. For the first time since his arrest Victor had the space and tranquility to start thinking and planning.

CHAPTER 10

In November 1988, after the first 35-meter leg of the tunnel was completed, three more diggers joined the group to make a total of nine — "nine companions of misfortune," as Jaime phrased it — and they divided into three teams. Each team would work for two hours, take four hours off to rest, and then put in another two hour shift.

Unfortunately, — Jaime remarked, — not everybody has the same physical capacity for tunneling. One of the new *compañeros* was too tall and became exhausted rapidly despite his dedication and will power. Another of the newcomers had been tortured with electricity and imprisoned. He had continuing nervous attacks and was particularly sensitive to lack of oxygen. We had to send him out to medical clinics frequently for EEGs and EKGs. The result was that even though we increased the number of workers by 50 percent, we didn't advance work on the tunnel by nearly that much. Nevertheless, the second segment of the tunnel forged ahead at the rate of about 1.35 meters per day.

One of the chief problems they had to contend with was the frequent occurrence of power blackouts all over Lima. Whenever this happened the workers had flashlights to provide minimal illumination, and they also rigged automobile headlights to an 8-volt battery, which gave them sufficient light to keep working. These improvisations, however, failed to resolve the most important problem: that of the ventilation system, which was totally dependent on the city power system. Whenever a power failure occurred, the diggers would spell each other every 15 or 20 minutes at the tunnel face and dig until their cheeks or foreheads started turning numb — a characteristic sign of oxygen starvation — or until they developed migraine headaches.

At one point they attempted installing an electric generator driven by a gasoline motor beneath the air shaft to provide current during the blackouts, but this proved impractical and dangerous because the motor made too much noise and gasoline fumes permeated the tunnel despite the exhaust tube leading up to the ground level. The machine was dismantled and hoisted back to the surface.

Despite these drawbacks, the digging proceeded steadily, and the new leg, christened *La Lucha Continua* (The Struggle Continues) inched its way toward Guard Tower 8. When it had progressed some 20 meters, however, the air extractor became less and less effective. It was still sucking air into the plastic tube at the tunnel face, but the flow of air from the ventilation duct to replace it grew more and more sluggish, and all the diggers experienced constant symptoms of oxygen starvation.

Armando was called in for consultation. He went to the tunnel face, filled his lungs with dead, sweaty air and realized the system was no longer performing its function. An analogy struck him: when the first MRTA tunnel from inside Canto Grande was discovered and the National Directorate decided it was unfeasible to tunnel out of the prison, they simply inverted the terms of the problem and decided to tunnel from the outside into the prison to rescue their comrades.

"Instead of sucking the dead air out," he told Jaime and the others, "let's try blowing fresh air into the tunnel face." They simply turned the extractor fan around and converted it into a blower fan. It worked like a charm, and from then on the diggers worked in a fresh-air environment. By the time the tunnel extended 100 meters underground, the air flow slowed down once more, but this time the problem was solved swiftly by installing a second, booster fan at the 100-meter mark, which picked up the air flow from the first fan and pushed it onward to the tunnel face.

"What sort of communications system did you have between the safe-house keepers above ground and the people working in the tunnel itself?" we asked Jaime.

"There was a triple electrical switch at the front door to control the porch light and the living room lights. We disconnected the porch light and ran the wiring into the tunnel where it terminated in a small, red bulb. When Paloma answered the front door, she would switch on the red light if she felt the visitors represented a security risk, and all underground work would stop until she switched it off."

"And how did you fill the hours when you were working underground? What did you talk about?"

"There was always plenty to talk about, and our voices carried back and forth through the tunnel. We recounted our experiences as guerrillas. Some of the *compañeros* had been up in the mountains, and we could almost fill our lungs with the fresh, cold air of the Andes even if the temperature in the tunnel was body temperature. Others of us had worked in the urban guerrilla, and we all had our share of close escapes.

"And then, of course, there were endless love stories that turned out well or badly. Most of them badly. A revolutionary militant doesn't often have an opportunity to settle down, get married and raise children. We have to snatch opportunities that most people find in the ordinary course of living. One of the *compañeros* was married and had a small daughter he was crazy about. He hardly talked about anything else, and when I had to leave the safe-house to help choose the larger pickup truck we needed, he had me mail a letter to his wife and daughter.

"A lot of the conversation was about political matters. We had the underground library, and it was well-stocked with books: political essays, mostly of a Marxist-Leninist nature, novels by Latin American writers with a progressive slant, books about the guerrilla experience in Latin America, such as Omar Cabezas' testimony, poetry by such writers as Pablo Neruda. And we all had access to the daily newspapers and news magazines when we were off work. Also, events in Eastern Europe were at boiling point while we were working on the tunnel. The Berlin wall was torn down while we were underground, for example, and these events formed the basis for endless discussion and argument."

"With so many people living and working together for months on end, didn't you end up getting on each other's nerves?" we asked him.

"Of course that happened," he replied. "The safe-house was cramped as more and more diggers came in to help with the job, and the tunnel was even more cramped with people squeezing past each other to get on with their different jobs. It was inevitable that there were quarrels and disagreements. Many of the *compañeros* were affected by the abnormal conditions, the crowding, by apparently trivial matters such as the uncouth eating habits of others. At night, for instance, there were roll-up mattresses and bodies in every room in the house and in all the corridors as well. For another thing, we only had a single toilet, and with the basically unhealthy working conditions there were frequent epidemics of diarrhea and urgent lines forming at the outhouse door. But despite all the difficulties, the illness, the personal disagreements and conflicts, we had one great solvent that eased such problems, and that was the necessity of getting on with the job, with finishing the tunnel, with being able to report to the National Directorate: 'Mission accomplished.'

"In fact, we had a slogan — a standing joke — that we repeated whenever tempers became overheated. One of the disputants, or any bystander, would raise a hand and say: 'Remember the morale, *compa*, keep up the morale.'"

As the house grew more crowded, housekeeping discipline became more and more important. All the occupants ate on plastic plates and used plastic drinking cups to avoid the sound of clattering dishes. Each individual washed his own dishes and utensils and hid them away in a pantry cupboard. Everybody washed and hung out his own clothing, and the high walls of the back patio concealed the abnormal amount of washing on the clothesline. All the diggers had to keep their voices down while above ground, despite the fact that the radio or television was constantly going. In the first weeks of her stay at the safe-house, Paloma discovered two guards lurking just outside the garage door next to the water tank. She presumed they were spying on the safe-house or listening for unusual sounds. She opened the garage door and questioned them as a normal housewife would. They confessed that they were using the shelter provided by the water tank and the wall to change out of their uniforms into civvies, as they were going off duty. They also asked her permission to leave their knapsacks behind the water tank while they were in Canto Grande.

"What do you keep in there?" Paloma asked, fearful of a planted bomb.

"It's food, *señora*, that we're taking home," one of the guards opened his knapsack to show her the contents. Naturally, it was food stolen from the prisoners daily allotment — a small example of the widespread corruption that existed among the prison guards and officials.

We asked Paloma about the interpersonal frictions that arose and how they were resolved.

There were frictions — she admitted — because the space seemed to shrink as more and more diggers crowded in. People's characters altered and grew edgy because of the nature of the work, because of physical fatigue and the psychic tension of knowing we might be discovered at any moment. But we managed to reach a level of understanding. We held regular meetings to analyze why the work wasn't going well, what was wrong, what was the solution. We ourselves were the protagonists and we had to come up with alternative solutions and decide which was the best.

Paloma herself — she confessed to us — was the occasional target of complaints from the others. Sometimes she over salted the food, or, even worse, she miscalculated the quantities necessary to feed the growing number of hungry diggers and everyone wound up with short rations. This was not a matter of economic necessity, because there was always sufficient money for the food budget, but simply of bad planning on her part.

Armando, an irregular visitor to the safe-house, was a sharp-eyed critic of the security system that inevitably grew more lax as the weeks and months passed, each day filled with the same deadly routine. He pointed out obvious security flaws on each visit and received promises that the problem would be corrected, but on the next visit he saw that the promises had not been kept. It became obvious that sterner measures were necessary to correct the situation and, with the concurrence of the National Directorate, he arrived at the safe-house unexpectedly one day and announced that a police inspection of each house in the neighborhood was underway and, with luck, the occupants might have five or ten minutes before the police knocked on the door.

There was a flurry of activity as the diggers readied their weapons to withstand a police attack and scurried about to hide all evidences of their existence. One of them dropped a pistol that clattered on the floor. Paloma checked the kitchen to make sure that surplus plates and utensils were hidden from view. Ten minutes went by and still the back room that concealed the tunnel entrance was not ready to pass inspection. Nearly 20 minutes after the announcement, Armando announced that the whole episode had been an emergency drill to test security measures and that the police were really not on the way.

We opened the door to inspect the room — he recalled — and some of the diggers still hadn't gotten into the shaft. They had decided to stay there and and were going to burst out shooting policemen. Then we held a general inspection. There were papers on the floor listing the safe-house rules, work schedules, measurements of how far the tunnel had advanced each day. There were even plates of half-eaten food because the drill took place during the lunch hour. There were sleeping bags half-hidden. We pointed out all the errors that had been committed and how each of them had to be resolved. We held a critique of all security aspects in a session that lasted several hours. At the end, we decided to suspend digging operations for an entire day and, instead, devote it to clearing up the security hazards. After that, I believe, the house could have passed routine police inspection, but not a check. The reason everyone was armed was in case the police obtained concrete data about the project and mounted a full-scale operation against the safe-house. In that case, everyone would have to come out firing, and of course the whole project would have come to an end.

Armando's fire drill was the greatest trauma the safe-house occupants had experienced until that time, and it had a sobering effect on all of them. Not long after, however, another security scare occurred when one of the diggers who was emptying sacks of dirt into the *camioneta*, which was parked in the enclosed patio, looked up to see a man watching him from atop a telephone pole across the street.

He completed the job normally and strolled into the kitchen to alert Paloma, who was preparing the midday meal. She went out the garage door, heart palpitating, and began talking to the peeping tom on the telephone pole. He turned out to be an electric company lineman who was installing street lights in the neighborhood, and he wasn't the least bit curious about trucks being loaded with dirt in somebody's inside patio.

That incident had been the most serious security threat yet, but there were others to come.

CHAPTER 11

The first occupants of the Canto Grande *venusterio* after its conversion into the prison's maximum-security pavilion were Osmán Morote, second in command of the *Sendero Luminoso*, and Victor Polay, head of the MRTA. The *venusterio* was located on the second and third floors of a pavilion next to the admissions building at the entrance to the prison. The ground floor was taken up with the *Republicano* guards' bunk room and day room and the processing center for visitors. Polay and Morote were assigned separate rooms opening onto a corridor some eight meters long on the topmost third floor. Victor's room had a private bath and a small window which let in the sun for several hours each morning and gave him a limited view of the central patio.

The Minister of Justice personally oversaw Polay's transfer from the cramped punishment cell to his new quarters, and Victor took advantage of the occasion to point out that he had the same right of access to the prison patio as the other prisoners, so he could exercise and take the sun each day. The Minister agreed with him in principle but left no written orders to that effect. The two prisoners were confined to their rooms for the first several weeks, until Victor raised the issue with the prison commandant.

"You have no right to hold us in solitary confinement, because neither of us has committed any infraction of prison regulations," he said. The commandant replied that the two of them were being isolated for their own protection, that if they were allowed to mingle with the other prisoners they might be exposed to physical aggression or assassination by unspecified political enemies.

"At least, we must have the right to use the corridor outside our cells," Victor insisted. "There is no physical danger there, and we are two civilized beings who will not spring at each other's throats."

When he was returned to the third floor, Victor refused to enter his cell and be locked up again. The commandant was reluctant to use force, and the principle was established that his and Morote's cell doors would be left unlocked during the day.

There were eight cells on the third floor — Victor explained — four on either side of the corridor, at the end of which was a barred doorway leading to an empty room and the stairway, which was closed off by another barred door. Morote occupied the end cell, and I was in the third cell on the same side, so we were separated from each other by an empty cell.

"What was your relationship with each other?" we asked him. "Did the two of you speak? Did you make friends with him?"

We maintained a respectful deference to each other: "Good morning." "Good afternoon." "How are things going?" "Just fine." He was a peculiar person who hardly ever came out to the corridor. He even received visitors behind the closed door of his cell. Besides, the *Senderistas* don't consider the MRTA to be a revolutionary organization, but rather their principal enemy and an agent of imperialism. To them, we are an armed revisionist group and for that reason more dangerous than their other enemies. They boast that they squash revisionists and reformists like cockroaches. With that sort of ingrained attitude on his part, there wasn't much room for a normal relationship.

The prison food was thin potato soup served once a day, and from the beginning, both Polay and Morote refused to touch it for fear it might be poisoned. They insisted that their three meals a day be prepared by trustworthy members of their own political groups. After they had left their plates untouched for several days, the prison officials conceded this point to avoid the situation taking on the aspect of a hunger strike. In the beginning, however, they insisted that the food be delivered to the first floor of the building, whence a *Republicano* would carry it up to the third floor. Both men objected to this on the grounds that the guard might slip poison into the food on the way upstairs. Prison authorities grudgingly conceded that the objection might be valid and, after the food trays were inspected, the couriers were searched for written messages, and allowed to deliver the meals in person to the third floor. A guard stood by to make sure that no conversation passed between the parties. Victor made it a habit to offer the guards a cigarette, a bit of fruit from his plate or the chance to leaf through a magazine the emissary had brought with him as a tacit reward for the chance to say "Hello," "How's everything?" "What's new?" and gradually the surly, suspicious attitudes relaxed.

You have to gain each small advance with patient persistence — Victor explained. — You win thirty seconds of conversation one week, a full minute the next. For another thing, the guards in the *venusterio* were changed at frequent intervals to prevent us from befriending them and possibly bribing them to help us escape. When the new guards come in, you behave as if it is customary and approved by the authorities to chat with the person who brings you your food, to ask him how the other *compas* are doing, how the artisan workshops are getting along, what's happened with the table and chair that Ciro was making for me?

And of course it was always Pedro who brought Polay his breakfast and lunch each day, while the women prisoners of the MRTA prepared and delivered his evening meal: Pedro, the shy, unassuming *compa* who never stood out amongst his companions, who never took the lead in organizing MRTA activities, and who always obeyed the guards' commands unquestioningly; Pedro, who was intelligence chief for the MRTA inside the prison and one of the few who knew about the tunnel that was creeping toward Canto Grande day by day, the mole hole on which their hopes of liberation rested. With access to Victor's cell twice a day, Pedro served as liaison between the MRTA leader in his solitary cell and Rodrigo, his chief lieutenant in Pavilion 2-A.

Before his arrest, Victor and the National Directorate had approved the tactic of lulling the *Republicanos* into believing that the political prisoners in 2-A had accepted their lot resignedly and wanted only to serve out their terms quietly and as comfortably as possible until they were released. By the time Polay arrived, all MRTA members had their own chests for storing personal effects, they had organized football, basketball, and ping-pong teams, and were busily producing woven baskets, toys, shoes, and carpentry products which they sold to improve their daily diet and living conditions. One of Victor's first orders was to further lull the guards by spreading the rumor that the MRTA prisoners were counting on negotiations with the Peruvian government to achieve a general amnesty for all its membership. They were to assume a relaxed, unpreoccupied attitude because they were confident they would be released by Christmas.

Victor and the National Directorate had also shaped the strategy of occupying the ground floor of Pavilion 2-A in order to give the MRTA access to the eventual tunnel opening.

When I was still free, we had given the order for a group of companions to start sleeping in the patio. We were thinking of the tunnel, of course, and we had to consolidate our presence on the ground floor, which was still precarious. We had them build walls in one corner and install a bathroom to create the impression that we were immovable and there to stay. All of this took time. Another thing we had to do was to expel ten common prisoners, all of them drug addicts who spent their time bothering the rest. The *compas* seized them and threw them out of the pavilion. They armed themselves with lances, chains, and knives. When the Republicans tried to enter, our people started negotiating, claiming that the presence of the ten was intolerable because they were drug addicts, they bothered family members on visiting days, they were constantly stealing from the other prisoners and creating problems. The guards accepted our arguments, and that consolidated our presence in the patio. We also carried out a very delicate political plan with the common prisoners who remained, dividing them into two opposing groups and maintaining friendly relations with both groups so that we held the balance of power.

Besides our constant exploration of the underground ducts, we had to carry out an intelligence plan with all the prison guards. Who were they? What were their characteristics? We drew up psychological profiles of each of them. We charted the movements of the prison personnel, the hours that shifts changed, what they did after they went off duty, depending on the weather and the day of the week. We also studied the behavior of all the common prisoners, and on the basis of all this data we drew up an operational plan for the escape.

"Were you allowed to receive visitors on the same basis as the other prisoners?" we asked.

Yes — Victor replied. — My mother, father, and brothers came to visit me. For security reasons it wasn't advisable for my wife and children to come to Canto Grande. During that time, the MRTA was involved in many operations, and it would have been terribly dangerous for them. We had captured Enrique Fereira, one of the "twelve apostles," as we call the heads of the twelve most important economic groups in the country.

There were other kidnappings, including that of a very important person: Heberto Salgado Palma, a presidential adviser and owner of TV Channel Five and Radio Programs of Peru. My family had received threats, despite the fact that my father was a founder of APRA and Alan García always invited him to participate in public party events. Of course, he wanted to set our family members against each other, but when my father made public declarations, he always said: "My son is not an *Aprista*. I don't share his ideas but I approve his behavior. I respect his ideals and the fact that he is struggling for social betterment."

By way of contrast, my mother is an *Aprista*, from an *Aprista* family, but she says: "No. I'm a socialist and I share my son's ideas. The only thing I ask of him is that he not abandon the struggle, that he act consistently with his ideals." I don't know whether it's because she has undergone ideological development or whether it's because of her mother's heart that she has turned socialist. She has always played the most important role in the family. When my father was in prison and when he was engaged full-time in political activities, she was the one who resolved all our economic and material problems.

Polay and Morote were not to have the *venusterio* to themselves for very long, however. An army general, implicated in narcotics trafficking, soon moved into two cells on the second floor, to be followed by a colonel who had been head of the Anti-Kidnapping Division, also on drug charges, and finally two majors and two captains of the Republican Guard, who were charged with aiding a number of wealthy narcotics bosses to escape from Lurigancho Prison. Canto Grande's perennial problem of progressive overcrowding was making itself felt in the maximum-security pavilion. In addition, prison trusties were assigned to the second and third floors to clean the cells, sweep the corridors, and run errands for the *Republicanos* and the prisoners themselves. These were informers, of course, who had been evicted from other pavilions under threat of death because of their betrayal of other prisoners to the authorities.

This was a nuisance — Víctor recalled — because we had to be careful of what we said. As in every other prison, the very walls have eyes and ears. It's incredible, but they listen to everything you say; they're glued to the walls. They spend hours sitting and watching everything you do. Besides, stool pigeons are excellent empirical psychologists. They know if you're up to something, if you're hiding something. They study your reactions, subtle changes in your behavior.

The Republicans also try to work on you: "Look, *comandante*, I really admire you. If you want to send a message outside, to your family, to anyone else, just let me know."

You can't trust anybody inside, but at the same time you can't close up with them. You have to talk with all of them, get to know them and decide to what extent they can be of help to you.

Bit by bit, with infinite patience, Victor set about amplifying the living space permitted him. The initial restrictions were eased, and he was permitted to go to the patio, accompanied by a guard, to take the sun and exercise. He was not permitted to mingle with the military prisoners on the second floor, but he had a television set and the others didn't in the beginning. Victor invited them to share his set to watch football matches, news programs, motion pictures, provided they could get the permission of the guard to open the gate between the second and third floors. In reciprocation they invited him to lunch with them on the second floor, with each prisoner providing his own food, and they convinced the guard to open the stairway gate and allow Victor to join them for leisurely lunches and conversation afterwards.

Victor took special pains to cultivate the general's friendship.

He was a cultured person, very interesting, and we started exchanging books. He had been a Sword of Honor, had won a gold plaque in the Military Academy. Then he'd advanced rapidly, always the first to be promoted. I think he made general at age forty-eight.

As the second floor cells became crowded with two and three officers to a cell, the general complained to the Canto Grande commandant that he didn't have sufficient space to receive his visitors, and why weren't some of the third floor cells used to ease the crowding on the second floor? The commandant agreed, after consulting his two prize political prisoners, and the colonel moved upstairs to join Polay and Morote.

That was what I wanted — Victor told us — because it fit with my long-range plans. The colonel was a neurotic type, filled with fear. The common prisoners hated him because he'd had many of them put behind bars for kidnapping. It was a paradoxical situation, because the MRTA specialized in kidnappings, and here I was, rubbing shoulders with the founder and former head of *Divise*, the Anti-Kidnapping

Division. He was about fifty-five years old, and he was fascinated with any kind of game. So we started playing cards: a second-floor team against a third-floor team.

By this time, other military prisoners had moved up to the third floor to join the colonel in cells that were still vacant. The military men on both floors had to order all their meals from a small, improvised popular restaurant across the street from the entrance to Canto Grande, and this proved expensive. The problem, Victor saw, was that there was no space on the second floor where they could install a kitchen to cook their own food. So he suggested to the general that they should get permission from the commandant to install a cook stove in the empty room at the head of the stairs leading into the third-floor corridor. This was speedily accomplished, and cooking details from both floors occupied the new kitchen during much of the day. As Victor had foreseen, this was a constant annoyance to the guard who held the keys to the barred gate at the end of the corridor and the other one leading downstairs to the second floor. Within a week, by tacit consent of all concerned, the gate leading from the corridor into the kitchen was left open during the day, and the guard only had to open the stairway gate to permit second floor occupants to use the kitchen.

This was another important step forward — Victor smiled with satisfaction. — During the day, we not only had the freedom of the corridor, but we had access to the kitchen. We had won the corridor, a room, and a gate that remained open during the day.

Victor had been in prison for two months when disaster struck the MRTA. He was listening to an afternoon news broadcast when it was announced that a column of terrorists had been wiped out at Los Molinos in the center of Peru. He was stunned, couldn't believe his ears. Sixty *compañeros* of the MRTA had been killed with one stroke. But the evening TV news confirmed the story. There were the sixty cadavers laid out in a row, the pile of captured weapons, grenade launchers, munitions. Next day's newspapers published more grisly photos. A bulldozer scooped out a lengthy common grave, pushed dirt over the piled bodies and tamped it down so none of the relatives could give their dead a decent burial.

Those were terrible, isolated, solitary days — Victor shook his head slowly at the memory. — It was the worst tragedy that had ever struck the organization. The *compañeros* who died there had been with us in the *Tupac Amaru Libertador* campaign. We had spent a year and a half organizing the operation, and the principal leaders were all close friends. I had traveled to Huancayo precisely to make a series of decisions concerning the national campaign the party had approved. One of our columns was going to strike in the northeast, taking San José de Cisa. In the east, we were going to take the city of Contamana, and in Lima we were simultaneously going to take a police station. But these *compañeros* were going to strike the principal blow of the campaign, which was the taking of Tarma, the most important city in the center of Peru. The other strikes were accomplished successfully, but this column was wiped out at Los Molinos. The army took no prisoners; they executed all the prisoners and the wounded.

Three MRTA columns totaling seventy-five combatants from different sectors of the guerrilla front were to converge on Tarma, take the city, and hold a public meeting with the townspeople before withdrawing, dispersing, and melting into the landscape. The largest group had to march from the jungle area where they were accustomed to living at 500 meters above sea level to a part of the Andes where the altitude is 3000 meters. The long march took them approximately a month and when they arrived in the target area, they were exhausted, but they had an important mission to accomplish. They commandeered two trucks to make the final assault on the city, loaded half the combatants onto each truck, and headed for Tarma at 4 a.m. on 28 April 1989. It was their ill fortune that the two trucks drove squarely into the middle of two columns of government troops — two reinforced infantry companies — one on either side of the road. The trucks were stopped, and while an officer was inspecting the drivers' papers, other soldiers started inspecting the backs of the trucks to see what loads the trucks were carrying. The MRTA combatants came out firing their weapons in the pitch darkness. The melee continued for five hours, but the seventy-five MRTA fighters were outnumbered by 400 well-armed troops. When the fire-fight died down and the prisoners and wounded had been dispatched, sixty-one MRTA guerrillas lay dead, while a bare dozen managed to escape in the darkness.

A week later — Victor continued — the organization of Mothers of Los Molinos held a public memorial in the square where the cadavers had been exhibited. Some of the family members came to visit me as well. About five mothers and sisters of the fallen *compañeros* came to the *venusterio*, all of them dressed in black. When I saw them coming, I thought: What can I do? How can I console them? What can I say to them?

They entered the cell, and it was the most marvelous thing that has ever happened to me. They said: "*Compañero*, how are you? You poor thing, all alone here. How you must have suffered at this terrible blow!" Instead of me consoling them, they were consoling me. The mother of one of the dead told me: "*Compañero*, this is a terrible moment; my son was killed. But don't worry; we're together here." Then the sister of two *compañeros* who had fallen — one had been killed earlier, and the other was head of one of the columns at Los Molinos — said to me proudly, contentedly, "My family has given up martyrs to the party, but we're going to triumph." (Here Victor choked up, paused for a long moment to regain self-control, then continued slowly.) My voice broke, and I had to make an incredible effort, because there they stood, all of them firm, and I couldn't display my own weakness. I had to be on the same level as they were and talk to them, tell them that from today we were all members of one family forever, and that when the revolution triumphed, Peru's hospitals and schools would bear the names of these dead comrades. I felt a surge of fresh air, of renewed energy as I spoke. When they came in, dressed in black, I expected the most natural reactions — accusations, recriminations — but instead of that they had come to console me.

CHAPTER 12

Work on the second leg of the tunnel progressed slowly but
steadily throughout 1989. The routine was dull and
monotonous, and the days followed one another in gray
procession: breakfast, work, lunch, work, shower, dinner,
watch television, go to bed. The dogs were well-fed, fat, and
happy, according to Paloma, and they particularly enjoyed
the social hour after dinner when they watched television
programs alongside the diggers.

The capture and imprisonment of *Comandante* Rolando
(Victor Polay) created consternation in the safe house, and
its occupants responded with increased dedication to their
task. The chief impediment, as always, was the large number
of boulders that had to be pried free and disposed of or
chiseled away. Armando had seen to it that the team was
provided with miners' axes—short-handled Alpinist axes
with a pointed end and a broad end—but the people
working at the tunnel face soon learned that they preferred
to work with crowbars. The chisel end penetrated the
compacted sand and earth effectively to free the many
boulders, and the curved claw-hammer end released
cascades of earth from the top and sides of the
excavation. There were six diggers now, divided into two
teams of three each. Jaime was chief and in charge of one
team, while Jorge was second in command and in charge of
the other. It was recognized by everyone that more
manpower was needed to speed progress, but there were no
militants to spare in the Lima zone, and the National

Directorate had to issue a call to the regional fronts of the MRTA to send reinforcements to the capital for an unspecified task.

Paloma, a pretty, vivacious girl, was the only woman in the safe house, with triple responsibilities as the cook who prepared daily meals, the doctor who tended scratches, bruises, and minor ailments and the security warden who kept a sharp eye on the neighbors and the guard patrols that occasionally moved through the area. It was perhaps predictable that Jaime and Jorge should both fall in love with her, but this created ugly personal tensions between the two and a pervasive atmosphere of unease amongst the rest of the occupants. Antonio, who had overall responsibility for the entire project, became aware of the situation and saw that he would have to step in as mediator before things got out of hand.

I visited the safe house every Sunday to hold a weekly evaluation session with the entire team, and first I talked to Paloma alone. She told me that she felt a comradely affection for both *compañeros* but didn't want to become emotionally entangled with either of them. She seemed a bit enigmatic about this, and I suspected she was taking that position to avoid problems at the work site. We knew that Jaime had been living with a girl, but what with his term in prison and his assignment to the dig immediately after his release, he hadn't seen her, except briefly, for months. Jaime and Jorge were jealous of each other, and the other diggers told me they felt Jaime was taking advantage of his position as chief digger to find opportunities to pursue his courtship.

To make matters worse, Luis Angel — Paloma's supposed husband — had a macho reaction to the situation. He was married to another woman and had never courted Paloma himself, but he resented the fact that two other men were quarreling over his "wife," and he started treating her badly and trying to intervene in her personal affairs. He and Jaime also rubbed each other the wrong way, because Jaime had an impulsive, domineering character and a quick temper: traits that occasionally led him to overreach himself as chief of the dig.

Once he was sure of the basic facts, Antonio called the group together and reviewed the situation frankly with all of them. He stressed the overriding need for harmony and unity of purpose in completing the project and, after Paloma reiterated her position of neutrality and friendly comradeship with both rivals, Antonio suggested rules of behavior to minimize future frictions. Jaime and Jorge shook hands and agreed to bury their feud, and Luis Angel accepted the fact that Paloma was not his personal property. This worked...for a few months.

Jaime, however, continued to be a source of contention. He was continually anxious — frantic — to get ahead with the job, and the others complained that he was a ruthless slave driver, pushing them to the point of exhaustion, keeping them working overtime to fulfill their daily quotas. Antonio, the diplomat and mediator, agreed with him in principal but tried his best to persuade him that military discipline and barked orders were out of place underground and that Jaime would achieve better results if he were to conceal his mailed fist in a velvet glove.

Despite the ventilation system, the tunnel heated up again as spring arrived in October and the earth began absorbing the sun's rays. Once again the temperature at the extreme end of the dig rose above body temperature and the breathing of more than three or four men at the face not only raised the temperature but depleted the available oxygen. Shifts had to be shortened to two hours, with excavators spelling each other every half-hour.

December is midsummer in the Southern Hemisphere, and the sun's vertical rays brought the tunnel temperature up to over a hundred degrees Fahrenheit. As Christmas approached, the team looked forward to a Christmas break in their tedious routine, and the conversation underground turned to eager planning as to how each of them would spend their end-of-year vacation.

The National Directorate, however, had other issues to consider. The tunnel was seriously behind schedule, and the deadline for its completion was dictated by a political timetable. National elections were scheduled for April 1990, and if no candidate won a clear majority in the first round of voting, a run-off contest would take place in early July. The MRTA decided that the tunnel must be finished and the escape carried out before the new president took office. They feared a Conservative victory by novelist Mario Vargas Llosa and a consequent change in the status of MRTA prisoners from that of political prisoners with certain minimal rights to that of hostages of an iron-fisted regime that would vent its wrath on them for any politico-military activities carried out by the organization. For this reason, orders from the top command were curt and clear: there would be no suspension of digging over the Christmas holidays.

When Antonio broke the news to Jaime, the latter shook his head and said he couldn't possibly pass the word on to his men or their morale would plummet to zero and progress would deteriorate in similar fashion. Antonio returned to the Directorate to argue the case and won a grudging modification of the plan. Work would continue over the Christmas holidays, but on a two-shift basis. A third of the diggers would rotate on abbreviated vacations over a two-week period.

Meanwhile, Paloma began suffering from severe back pains that increasingly immobilized her and disrupted the cooking schedule and house chores while she lay suffering in bed, unable even to straighten her legs. Jaime assigned two off-shift diggers to take over her responsibilities, and the safe-house menu degenerated into improvised snacks and guerrilla campfire cooking.

Luis Angel took her to medical appointments, but the doctors prescribed only analgesics and bed rest. Paloma, a physician herself, knew these were palliatives and that something much more serious was the matter with her, something requiring extensive laboratory tests.

Uncle Felix was in the first group to leave the safe-house for an abbreviated Christmas vacation. Antonio met him in the center of Lima and gave him some pocket money and the operational funds to buy a new mine car, inasmuch as the one in use at the dig was on the point of collapse. The two made arrangements to meet again several days later, and they went their separate ways. Uncle Felix went home to his wife, relaxed for a day or two, and then decided to visit an old friend and former MRTA collaborator, the "Professor." The latter was a retired schoolteacher who lived by himself in a rooming house. He knew he had once been listed in police files as a probable subversive, but there were no serious charges pending against him, and he believed the security forces had forgotten about him, since he regularly appeared at the social security office each month to collect his pension check.

Another MRTA member had been picked up a few weeks previously, and under interrogation he HAD mentioned the Professor's name. On the appointed day of the month, the latter appeared with his son to pick up his check, and they were both arrested. The security forces staked out the Professor's room, and when Uncle Felix came calling on his old friend some days later, he was also scooped up by the police and taken to the offices of DIRCOTE.

When Uncle Felix missed his scheduled meeting with Antonio, the latter immediately contacted Felix's wife, who only knew that her husband had set off to visit the Professor and had not returned. Cautiously, avoiding the police trap, Antonio investigated and learned, to his consternation, that

Uncle Felix, who knew the entire history of the Canto Grande tunnel, was being held — and undoubtedly tortured — by the Anti-Terrorist Police. If the old man broke under interrogation, that was the end of the project on which so many hopes depended. Antonio hastily informed the National Directorate and received approval to evacuate the safe house. A few hours later, at his regular daily rendezvous with Luis Angel, he ordered the latter to close down the operational site immediately and to evacuate the entire team. He set up a new rendezvous point for a few hours later, and sent Luis Angel on his way.

Another emergency fire drill ensued, this time for real, as the occupants — there were 12 of them by now — hid tools, clothing, bedrolls and extra plates in the tunnel shaft and padlocked the door to the "extra bedroom." Luis Angel hurried over to *Señor* Aldaña's house to inform him that Paloma's back condition required her immediate hospitalization, and he would have to attend her during this period. He asked Aldaña to keep an eye on the house during their absence, but didn't offer to leave the house keys in the latter's keeping. Paloma, for her part, limped over to see the lady next-door, related the same cover story, and asked her to feed the animals while she was gone.

Antonio's contact in the National Directorate checked on the MRTA's available safe-house facilities in the Lima area, inasmuch as four of the diggers came from provincial areas of Peru and had no families who could put them up. The pickup truck, with Luis Angel and Paloma in the cab and 10 well-armed diggers concealed in the covered truck bed, made a street-corner contact with Antonio and the Directorate member and followed his car to a beach house overlooking the Pacific, where the out-of-town members of the team, led by Jorge, took up residence, while the rest dispersed to the homes of relatives and collaborators for a Christmas reunion.

The evacuation had been carried out without a hitch, and the team members welcomed the unexpected respite from their grubby underground existence. Jorge and his group bathed in the Pacific, jogged for miles along the sandy beach to stretch their leg muscles and played volleyball between meals. Paloma, relieved of her housekeeping duties, was able to follow doctor's orders and rest, in the hopes that this would relieve her condition.

Despite the change of scene and the opportunity for physical relaxation, nervous tension ran high in all members of the team because of the uncertainty as to whether or not Uncle Felix would break under torture and give away the tunnel secret. A few days after the evacuation, Antonio had Luis Angel round up the dispersed diggers and bring them to the beach house for a debriefing and general evaluation session.

He methodically reviewed the evacuation procedure to satisfy himself that no incriminating evidence had been left behind in the safe house, but when he asked who had replaced the lid on the tunnel shaft, he was met with a stunned silence. The lid that concealed the entrance was a heavy concrete slab with tiles set into the top to simulate the flooring in the rest of the house. Normally, it was left leaning against the wall behind the open shaft. Now, the realization slowly dawned that nobody had replaced it and the entrance lay gaping open to anyone who ripped the padlock off the bedroom door.

The responsibility for this grievous security breach was clearly Jaime's, who as chief of the team should have made a final inspection of each room before cramming into the pickup truck with the rest. Instead, they all recalled, his chief preoccupation had been to make sure that each of the diggers took his sidearm with him so that no weapons were left in the safe house.

This revelation brought down a renewed storm of criticism on Jaime's head. Everyone, it seemed, had been nursing grievances against him for his highhanded manner of directing the operation and for the stern punishments he handed out for infractions of work discipline. Obviously, Antonio's previous admonitions to him to change his working methods had been disregarded. Now Antonio turned to him and said:

"Look, Jaime, if there were just one or two *compañeros* who bore a grudge against you, that would be understandable. But with this many complaints, there must be some basis behind them. What do you say?"

Jaime, his pride hurt to the quick, responded in character:

"I say they're all a lazy bunch of clowns."

Antonio demoted him from leadership of the group on the spot, basically because of his security breach with respect to the tunnel lid, but also because of his failures as a leader to promote a harmonious work environment.

Jorge became the new team leader: an obvious choice, but one that rubbed salt in Jaime's psychic wounds. In addition, Paloma was secluded in a house where he could not see her, enduring the pain and agony of her undiagnosed illness. His demotion, which he was slowly assimilating, and Paloma's suffering weighed on him.

Jorge was soon to have problems of his own. One of the newcomers to the digging team was Carlos, who was presently under Jorge's immediate command at the beach house. Carlos was a taciturn young man who had been attached to one of the guerrilla columns in the mountains. He did his job, kept to himself, and discouraged attempts by the others to engage him in conversation. Between Christmas and New Year's, Antonio was contacted by another MRTA militant who had been a squad leader in Carlos's guerrilla column and who knew nothing about the tunnel project. He told Antonio that Carlos had just telephoned him to complain that he didn't like his present assignment and that he wanted to be transferred back to his guerrilla unit in the mountains.

Antonio was alarmed at the double breach of security. In the first place, it was strictly forbidden to make personal telephone calls, and secondly, the call had violated the military chain of command. Carlos should have voiced his request to Jorge, who would then pass it on to Antonio, and from there it would be relayed to the National Directorate.

Antonio made immediate contact with Jorge while the others were at the beach and outlined the problem to him. He instructed Jorge to confine the others to the beach house until the following morning when a meeting would be held to discuss the situation. Jorge passed on the order when the others returned from their outing. Carlos listened impassively, went to bed when the others did, and the following morning was nowhere to be found. He had slipped out sometime in the early morning hours and disappeared. As the hours went by without his return, suspicion became a certainty. He had not simply slipped out to make another forbidden phone call. It was unlikely that the police had picked him up in that sparsely inhabited area. The rest of the team had to face the numbing fact that Carlos, one of their sworn brothers, had deserted.

THE TIME TUNNEL-IV

World War I produced a flush of prosperity in Peru as the prices of its principal exports soared rapidly, and with them inflation. But in 1919, falling prices and shrinking exports created a crisis situation that discredited the oligarchic ruling class and brought Augusto B. Leguía to power on a platform that promised to modernize Peru and create a "New Homeland." Leguía borrowed heavily from U.S. bankers to finance a vast public works program and welcomed U.S. investment in railroads and in the copper mines of the Andes. An incipient labor movement made its appearance, strongly influenced by European anarcho-syndicalism, and two leaders of leftist thought appeared on the national scene to offer conflicting recipes for a Peruvian and Latin American revolution.

Victor Raúl Haya de la Torre first appeared on the Peruvian political scene as president of the Federation of University Students during the 1918 campaign for university reform. He was exiled by Leguía and appeared in Mexico in 1924 where, under the sway of Mexico's nationalistic revolution, he founded a continent-wide anti-imperialist front christened the *Alianza Popular Revolucionaria Americana* (APRA). This popular-front movement embraced not only the Latin American left-labor unions, indigenist movements, and intellectuals, but even included the nationalistic, anti-American bourgeois sectors of society.

Haya de la Torre was an impassioned, charismatic speaker and a polemical writer with a strong "man on horseback" streak. He idolized Lenin and the small group of disciplined conspirators who had achieved the Bolshevik revolution, and he envisioned himself as the anointed *caudillo* who would carry out the Latin American revolution. He was essentially a political activist, impatient with theorizing but ever ready to use ideological argumentation as a tactical weapon to overcome his opponents.

José Carlos Mariátegui was one of Latin America's most incisive Marxist thinkers and activists. He spent his formative political years in Europe, preoccupied with the problem of how to adapt European Marxist theory to the special conditions of Peru, where an urban proletariat—the indispensable motor of the communist revolution—was still virtually nonexistent, and the ignorant masses of Indian peasantry were the overwhelming national reality. Mariátegui thought he had found the missing link in the communal cooperative traditions of the indigenous peasantry that had been handed down from the time of the Inca empire, and he theorized that the organization of the copper miners' union in the Peruvian highlands could serve as the entering wedge to educate and indoctrinate the peasant masses over a period of time and eventually create a peasant-labor alliance (under the hegemony of the latter) that would achieve the revolution.

In 1928, Haya de la Torre converted the APRA from a continental front into a Peruvian political party that supposedly would carry him to the presidency with mass backing for his revolutionary political program. Mariátegui, who had previously maintained friendly, cooperative relations with the *Apristas*, rejected Haya's plan to impose a revolutionary vanguard from above with himself as predestined leader. Mariátegui demolished the theoretical foundations of *Aprismo*, foreseeing, with prophetic exactitude, that at any revolutionary juncture, the bourgeois elements in the party would opt for imperialist domination and preservation of property rights.

After founding the Socialist party, Mariátegui died of a lingering illness in 1930 at the age of thirty-five, and Haya de la Torre was able to establish the hegemony of the Peruvian left under the APRA banner.

The Socialists, under the leadership of Eudocio Ravines (who was later to become virulently anticommunist) took an ultra-leftist stance that effectively alienated intellectuals and moderates and drove them toward the APRA in increasing numbers. A spontaneous insurrection by APRA militants took place in Trujillo in 1932 while Haya was in jail. The uprising was brutally repressed and the APRA outlawed. From that point on, the movement gradually lost its anti-imperialist, revolutionary thrust, and Haya, who had become a staunch anticommunist, transformed it into a populist, vaguely social-democratic, party that retained its hold on the popular imagination despite Haya's opportunistic maneuverings that, years later, led him into military conspiracies and even into a pact with the forces of the dictator Odria.

CHAPTER 13

The MRTA ringleaders inside Canto Grande — Victor Polay, Rodrigo, Ciro, and one or two others — realized that the crucial problem they had to solve was how to bring the women prisoners from the second floor of the admissions building and Victor himself from the third floor of the *venusterio* to the ground floor of Pavilion 2-A, which by now was under MRTA control. Once the tunnel emerged, the three separate groups had to be brought together with split second timing and disappear through the tunnel before the Republican guards realized what was happening.

Victor, confined in the maximum-security pavilion surrounded by guards and stool pigeons day and night, considered and rejected several possible solutions. He knew, from his daily briefing by Ciro, that an exploratory team was opening an escape route for the women prisoners through the subterranean ducts curving from admissions to 2-A. They had obtained or made keys to open most of the grilled doors that barred their way and were seeking solutions to the remaining problems they faced. Victor was satisfied that they would find the answers by the time the tunnel had reached its terminal point.

Once it opened, weapons would be handed up to the prospective escapees so that in case of discovery they could fight a rearguard action to cover the people who were streaming to freedom. This created a possibility for the MRTA to take the central patio of Canto Grande by armed force while they sent a rescue team to free Victor from his third-floor cell. Such a course would be a desperate, last-ditch measure which Victor found repellent. It would inevitably involve shooting and bloodshed, and worst of all it would mobilize all Peruvian security forces to close a dragnet around Canto Grande before the rest of the escapees could make their getaway. What he wanted was a clean jailbreak with no violence on either side, in which all forty-eight inmates would disappear as if by sleight of hand.

While Victor pondered alternatives to a violent breakout, a significant change took place on the first floor of the *venusterio*. The ground floor had remained empty while the second and third floors were modified to become the maximum security area of the prison. Victor knew that prison authorities were considering a proposal to convert it into a storage room for prison food supplies, and there was even a plan under consideration to turn it into a sort of general store, run by the prison administration, where prisoners could buy supplementary rations that the state was supposed to provide them but which were not forthcoming. This idea, however, was discarded as being so blatantly corrupt that it could not withstand the most superficial investigation.

Finally, through connivance and possible bribery, the ground floor was allocated to Reynaldo Rodríguez, the most notorious drug trafficker in all Peru: a man who had amply earned his nickname, "the Godfather." The Godfather was incarcerated in Pavilion 3-A with all the rest of the convicted drug dealers. He had spent his time in prison perfecting his knowledge of criminal law and now, as a means of currying favor amongst the prison population and the general public, he took over the ground floor of the *venusterio* and converted it into an Office of Juridical Studies that offered free legal advice to Canto Grande prisoners, the great majority of whom could not afford to consult a lawyer regarding their rights or possibilities of appeal. Within a few days of the opening, a constant stream of prisoners crowded the new offices.

This development alarmed the imprisoned army officers on the second and third floors when Victor pointed out to them that there was only one guard on duty on the first floor to control the multitude of common prisoners seeking advice. The general and colonel took the lead in seeking an audience with the commandant to express their concerns for their own safety, with the general serving as spokesman for the group.

He pointed out that it would be relatively easy for one or more common prisoners with a grudge to overpower the single guard and use his keys to gain access to the second and third floors — Victor said. — He demanded that the permanent third-floor guard be moved down to the first floor to support the other guard and that the barred access door to the stairway be kept permanently locked. Furthermore, the general added, the guards themselves were not trustworthy and frequently abandoned their posts during the night to go out in the patio and smoke marijuana or cocaine paste with their companions.

The commandant agreed that the increased security measure was probably necessary, but in that case who would control the keys to the second and third floors that gave access to the kitchen?

"Simple," the general snorted. "Give them to your stool pigeon here. He's your man, and he's on duty twenty-four hours a day to keep an eye on us."

And so it was settled. The trusty, known as "Mikito" to the rest, became custodian of the keys, and his new role inflated his sense of self-importance. This development also favored Victor's long-range escape plans, and he subtly began flattering the trusty's sense of self-esteem and giving him tips for such small favors as opening the gate leading to the second floor.

One morning the prisoners of *Sendero Luminoso* started a noisy demonstration in Pavilion 4. As they clanged pots and pans against the barred doors and windows and shouted slogans of defiance, the prison security forces went to full alert, and a detachment of Republican guards, armed with combat rifles, came storming up the stairway of the *venusterio*. Victor happened to be in the kitchen, making a pot of coffee, and he watched, fascinated, as they stopped at the landing on the far side of the grilled door that closed off the stairway to the second floor. They had brought a short ladder with them, and one of them mounted it, unlocked a padlock that secured the skylight in the ceiling, and pushed it open. The others followed him to take up combat positions on the roof, and they remained there until the rioting died down.

That was an illumination — Victor recalls. — I had always assumed that the skylight was solidly fixed into the ceiling, but now I realized it was a possible escape avenue onto the roof. From then on, I studied it closely every time I was invited down to lunch on the second floor. The *compañeros* in 2-A had a clear view from their fourth floor balcony, and they drew a sketch for me, showing that the roof of the *venusterio* was connected to Pavilion 6-B by a steep, almost vertical ramp. But I felt I had to see the exact layout for myself.

By now, there were three television sets operating in the *venusterio*, and three television antennae jutting above the building. Selected prison employees were allowed on the roofs at certain hours to open and close the valves that provided each pavilion with water for a half-hour daily. Armed guards in the eight towers closely observed all movement there during the day, but refrained from shooting. From 6 p.m. on, however, it was a different story, and the guards were under orders to train their searchlights and open fire on anyone spotted against the skyline. Despite the possibility of sudden death, some of the common prisoners were accustomed to prowling the rooftops at night, seeking entry into other cellblocks to steal whatever could be carried away.

Victor passed the word to Rodrigo to contract one of these expert burglars to steal the three television antennae, and a few mornings later they were gone. The general and the colonel, plus Victor himself, registered a strong protest with the commandant at this intolerable sneak-thievery and placed orders for three new antennae. When they were delivered a week later, Victor undertook to supervise the Republican guards in their installation and directional aiming to achieve the clearest possible images. Guards set up the ladder on the landing and unlocked the skylight to clamber onto the roof. When they had mounted and connected the antennae, Victor turned on his set to pick up the signals. Then he climbed the ladder, pushed his head through the open skylight, and ordered the guards to swivel the directional antennae one way or another for clearer reception, after which he returned to his cell to see whether the image had improved. He deliberately prolonged the process until he had verified the existence of the steep ramp leading to Pavilion 6-B and assured himself that it was a feasible escape route. While on the ladder, he also inspected the padlock and discovered that the hasp was anchored into a weak mixture of cement and could be pried free with nothing more than a strong screwdriver.

Mikito, the stool pigeon, was an alcoholic and a drug addict, as were almost all of the common prisoners. His new position of authority as turnkey for the maximum-security pavilion went to his head, and the tips that Victor and the others gave him for small services enabled him to indulge his two vices. The more he drank, the more arrogant he became.

It was at this time that the MRTA kidnapped Hector Delgado Parker, one of Alan García's closest advisers and head of Television Channel 5 and Radio Programs of Peru, the largest broadcast chain in the country. In a daring daylight assault, an MRTA commando team halted his armored Mercedes Benz, weakened a bulletproof window with automatic weapons fire, and smashed through the window with a sledgehammer. Delgado Parker received two bullet wounds and left bloodstains on the back seat of the car. In the public hullabaloo that followed, the news media immediately assumed that the television magnate had been sequestered in order to negotiate the exchange of his freedom for that of Victor Polay. Inside Canto Grande, the prison grapevine spread rumors concerning the impending exchange and even Mikito, the stool pigeon, began fantasizing. Victor recalls the incident with amusement.

Everybody says you're leaving, Victor, he told me and you're going to take me with you. I talked to the *comandante* about it, and he said: "If he orders you to go with him, you're going to have to go." But if you take me, you'll have to take one or two of the other boys as well.

I was amused and told him not to worry; if there was an exchange I promised I'd take him with me. Mikito suddenly became an enthusiastic revolutionary and started wearing a sort of scapulary on his chest, with a drawing of Che Guevara on one side and Tupac Amaru on the other.

Alan García appealed to the MRTA to give Delgado Parker proper medical attention, but by that time a team of MRTA doctors had already extracted the two bullets in an operation performed in the "people's prison" where he was being held, and the patient was on the road to recovery.

Meanwhile, the tunnel was advancing and we were counting the rate of advance each week and demanding more speed, longer hours, more diggers on the job. At times we were unreasonable, and we'd get the reply that they were doing the best they could under existing conditions. But we had good reason to keep up the pressure on the tunnelers: we anticipated that if Vargas Llosa won the elections, our conditions would change drastically, the *compañeros* in 2-A would be dispersed throughout other Peruvian prisons, and I would probably be sent to a military prison.

Victor continued sending and receiving operational messages via Pedro, who was now bringing him three meals a day. Delgado Parker was eventually ransomed by the MRTA and the anticipated exchange never took place. But in December 1989, a shootout took place between army troops and an MRTA guerrilla encampment on the Eastern Front, and Victor's situation took a critical turn.

We had an important encampment there with a good many *compañeros* undergoing military training. A number of the students were killed, while those wounded and taken prisoner were summarily executed by the military troops.

The MRTA has always respected the laws of war, and when we took a town or military post we respected the rights of the wounded and prisoners. But the army had always refused to reciprocate, so now the National Directorate decided the time had come to sanction the man responsible for these crimes: Gen. Enrique López Albujar, who had been commander-in-chief of the army and Peru's first Minister of Defense. An MRTA commando team located and executed him, and the organization announced that it had been an act of elementary justice; that it was not an MRTA tactic to assassinate generals, but, in this case, a response to concrete facts.

This action created an atmosphere of tension inside the prison, because the newspapers started claiming that the order to execute López Albujar originated in Canto Grande, that it was Polay's act of revenge. Obviously, I was in prison, and you cannot telephone a politico-military organization from a prison cell. The decision was made by the party leadership and was not my personal responsibility.

The tension increased when an army detachment appeared outside the walls of Canto Grande and took up combat positions. Inside, there was a general attitude that something was brewing and that we were going for the general's death. Besides, from the very first day I arrived, I was made aware of the fact that I was being held as a hostage. I kept insisting that I be transferred to Pavilion 2-A with the rest of the *compañeros*. It was the only spot where I would really feel safe. If anyone tried to kill me there, they would have to kill all of us, whereas in the *venusterio* at any time a couple of Republican guards could walk into my cell, string me up to the window bars, and claim I had hanged myself. Or dress me in a uniform, drag me out to no-man's-land, and put a bullet through my head, claiming I had tried to escape.

Intuitive foreboding spreads like wildfire through a prison. When there's going to be a prison riot, for example, a silence descends over the whole place as people seek their places, and suddenly it explodes. Or when they are going to kill someone, you can sense it in the atmosphere and people start avoiding the prospective victim. There's a prison saying: "He stinks of death." After the death of López Aguja, I sensed that oppressive atmosphere, felt the others were avoiding me, that the attitude of the Republican guard was subtly different. We of the MRTA were stinking of death, but we kept on behaving as if nothing had happened, kept on with the activities of exploration and reconnaissance, but with greater caution than ever.

Meanwhile, the behavior of Mikito, the stool pigeon, grew more and more intolerable. Victor humored his pecadillos and subtly flattered his ego, but the former INPE colonel and one of the majors had a serious falling-out with him, and the final straw came when, during a visiting day, Mikito got drunk and started threatening the visitors: an unforgivable prison sin.

As luck would have it, this breach of etiquette occurred shortly after a new prison commandant, nicknamed "Comandante Chico," had taken over the reins at Canto Grande. All the occupants of the *venusterio* demanded an interview with him and insisted that Mikito be removed from the maximum-security area.

Comandante Chico didn't want any unnecessary problems during his first weeks on the job, and he gave in to their demands. Besides, Mikito was the former commandant's stool pigeon, not his, and he had no interest in the prisoner's fate. He also agreed that the INPE colonel should become custodian of the key to the barred doors on the third floor, since it was obvious to all prison officials by this time that the officers in the *venusterio* were chiefly concerned with locking themselves in for their own security rather than with trying to escape.

It irked the colonel and wounded his pride to have to serve as turnkey to the other prisoners. Within a short time, by mutual agreement, the third-floor occupants bought a new chain and padlock, to which they all had keys, and the door leading to the stairway was left open during the day. Victor was elated at this development, but of course he had to celebrate his triumph silently. Now the way lay open to the skylight on the third-floor landing and escape.

CHAPTER 14

Uncle Felix, after being held for interrogation in DIRCOTE longer than the legal fifteen days, was remanded to Canto Grande and reacted with surprise and indignation when Rodrigo asked him whether or not he had given away any information about the tunnel project under torture.

"Of course not," he snorted. "What kind of a greenhorn do you think I am?"

Carlos, the deserter, simply disappeared and was not seen again by anybody in the organization. Despite the risk he represented, the National Directorate decided that work had to be resumed, and on 19 January 1990, Paloma, Luis Angel, and Paloma's "cousin," María, returned to the safe house and inspected it, inch by inch. The tunnel entrance still yawned open behind the padlocked bedroom door, but nothing had been touched, they decided, and it was highly unlikely that the police had staked out the house to set a trap for the returnees. The rest of the team came back in the pickup truck under cover of darkness and the digging resumed.

When the tunnel was vacated just before Christmas, it was approximately a hundred meters long and was aimed directly at Tower No. 8 beside the main entrance to the prison. During the Christmas security hiatus, the National Directorate decided a major effort was necessary if the project were to be completed by the election deadline that had been set. Three new diggers were assigned to the team, to make a total of twelve, and the edict was issued that no one was to leave the project site until the tunnel had been completed and the *compañeros* in Canto Grande rescued.

Paloma's month-long rest had not improved her back problem, and X-rays taken during that period revealed that she had developed a disk hernia between two vertebrae that required a delicate operation. This was undoubtedly a consequence of lifting and tying endless sacks of dirt at the bottom of the tunnel shaft. By this time, she was bedridden almost all the time, and she explained to the neighbors that her cousin María had come to care for her until she could be hospitalized. María would then stay on, keeping house for her husband during and after the operation, until her return. A few days later, Luis Angel drove Paloma off for the long-delayed surgical intervention and María took over the cooking obligations for the enlarged team.

We had no trouble in selling this cover story to the neighbors — Paloma recalled — because it is true that María and I resembled each other a great deal; we looked like "family."

With the new diggers contributing to the excavation, the old Ford pickup truck was unable to carry away all the dirt that accumulated. It was overloaded and too slow, taking forty-five minutes to get to the dump site and an equivalent amount of time to return. Besides, thanks to Luis Angel's ignorance of proper maintenance procedures, it was constantly breaking down, and digging had to come to a stop when the tunnel entrance became choked with sacks of dirt. It was clear to all that the light pickup truck was the bottleneck that was slowing down the work.

Purchase of a new vehicle, however, was preceded by a cautious security evaluation and the fabrication of a cover story to allay the possible suspicions of neighbors and the Republican guard in case they became curious about Luis Angel's acquisition of a newer automobile. Since the old

Ford was worn out, the story went, Luis Angel had decided to trade it for a larger and newer Dodge pickup truck, and he made up the difference in price by borrowing from family members.

With three new diggers at work and the haulage problem resolved, work speeded up, and during February and the first half of March the tunnel advanced for the first time at the rate of one meter per day. Digging continued on Sundays, now that they were approaching the outer wall of the penitentiary, since that was a visitors' day at Canto Grande and prison guards were occupied all day long and less likely to detect sounds of underground digging. Monday was a day of rest for the entire team.

Paloma's operation was successful and she returned to the safe house, after a brief period of recuperation, to share the housekeeping chores with María. Circumstances forced another change in personnel. With increased quantities of dirt to carry and dump, Luis Angel required a helper to speed up the loading and unloading of the Dodge. One of the diggers, René — an experienced driver — was shifted topside to join the "family" of caretakers and was introduced to the neighbors as Luis Angel's cousin who had come to join him in his flourishing haulage business.

Victor Polay and the National Directorate were constantly demanding more speed in the construction of the tunnel to meet the July deadline they had set. Jorge, who had been promoted to chief of the crew, was not as exacting a leader as Jaime had been, and he and Jaime still bristled when they confronted each other. An added complication was that Jaime's courtship of Paloma was prospering, and Jorge was clearly piqued at this development.

Antonio, who had always been in overall administrative charge of the entire project, now made the move he had been itching to make for months. He petitioned the National Directorate to be relieved of his outside logistical and liaison duties so he could return to the safe house and take direct charge of the dig. A member of the Directorate replaced him, and in mid-March Antonio moved into the safe house. A few weeks later three new diggers joined the team to make a total of fifteen workers plus the "family" of four above ground, or an overall total of nineteen occupying the house, which was now bursting at the seams.

When Antonio arrived, the diggers had been divided into two groups of six each, and he immediately saw that the work was inefficiently organized and there were times when the crucial part of the work — the actual digging at the tunnel face — was neglected while most of the team engaged in timbering the overhead or smoothing and cementing the floor. Some of the workers would simply sit around and watch because there was no room in the low narrow excavation for them to take part in the job at hand.

Antonio held an evaluation session in which he pointed out that digging was the priority task that must go forward night and day, no matter what other underground tasks had to be accomplished. It was decided that each team would be divided into three specialized groups. Two diggers would work at the tunnel face, actually excavating dirt and rocks. Two others would sack the dirt and haul it in the mine car back to the entrance shaft.

The third group of two would work at timbering and stuccoing the overhead or at smoothing and cementing the floor. Each shift lasted three hours, and each team worked two shifts or six hours a day.

The new division of labor speeded up the digging and also increased the amount of dirt that had to be moved. But three hours of hard underground labor, followed by only a three-hour rest period and then another three-hour shift proved to be an exhausting routine for all concerned.

As each new increment of laborers arrived on the scene, they were given classes in digging by Jaime and Jorge and learned how to timber and stucco the overhead and smooth and pave the floors. From the outset they were assigned to teams of experienced diggers for practical, on-the-job training.

When three new recruits arrived at the beginning of April, Antonio divided the team into five groups of three persons each: one to dig, one to haul dirt, and one to timber and pave the tunnel. Shifts were reduced from three to two hours, and each team got four hours off after finishing their shift. This way, each team would put in either two or three shifts per day for a maximum of six hours labor and work went forward at the rate of fourteen hours per day.

The results were gratifying. The workers were well rested and accomplished more in fewer hours of work than they had before. Their output of dirt and rock to be hauled away increased appreciably, but the greater output created new bottlenecks. First came the shortage of sacks. The Dodge pickup had more than twice the carrying capacity of the previous Ford, but as the dirt piled up all the sacks were either on their way to the dump site or else filled with dirt and piled at the bottom of the entrance shaft and at the sides of the tunnel itself. Workers had to squeeze past the sacks to get to their work stations. The obstruction caused the air flow to diminish throughout the tunnel and the previous symptoms of oxygen starvation reappeared.

Antonio ordered 200 more sacks, which arrived a few days later, but now the expanded team was excavating a greater amount of sand and dirt, and in less than two months after its acquisition, it became clear that the Dodge's capacity was insufficient to haul away the dirt that was accumulating. Luis Angel and his helper were limited for security reasons to making three trips a day to the dumpsite. When they left for "work" in the morning, the pickup was piled high with full sacks. They would make the necessary purchases of cement, timbering material, and food supplies, and return at noon. Paloma had accustomed the neighbors to this routine with the story that Luis Angel required a home-cooked dietary meal at midday because of his stomach ulcers. During the lunch hour, the Dodge was loaded again and took off for the dump site a second time. A third trip was made after dark, but still the sacks of dirt piled up and work frequently had to come to a stop after lunch because there was no place to store the excess.

With the Dodge constantly overloaded, we were limited to working fifteen hours a day, six days a week — Antonio explained. — There was no need to work longer, because it would have been in vain and we would simply clog the tunnel with sacks. Actually, we worked fourteen hours a day, because we lost ten or fifteen minutes every time the shifts changed. On our one day off each week, we organized classes of history and philosophy in the morning, and we spent the afternoon studying current events and the national political scene. It was during this time that the Eastern Europe bloc was starting to disintegrate, and these events plus Gorbachev's *perestroika* absorbed our attention.

The solution to the dirt problem was clearly to buy a full-sized truck, capable of hauling all the dirt excavated each day. This solution was doubly attractive because it would solve another problem that had worried the National Directorate: at the final moment, a covered truck could serve as the getaway vehicle for a majority of the escapees, whereas the Dodge pickup could only accommodate from fifteen to twenty individuals.

After considerable debate over the security risk the acquisition of a truck would represent, stern reality imposed itself: there was simply too much dirt to be moved and a larger vehicle was required if the tunnel were to advance at the pace required to free the MRTA prisoners by the July deadline. The National Directorate reluctantly acquiesced in the purchase.

Luis Angel paved the way for the change by letting the neighbors know that he was about to embark on a new venture of transporting heavy construction materials and was swapping the Dodge for a larger truck that one of his relatives had been using in the family haulage business. When the truck appeared at the safe house, the neighbors inspected it admiringly and accepted it as still another evidence of Luis Angel's untiring enterprise in building up his prosperous business.

Guerrilla organizations are always highly conscious of the time factor — Antonio told us — and at every step they try to analyze whether time is working in their favor or against them. In our particular situation, with a specific deadline to meet for the liberation of the *compañeros*, it was clear that time was working against us. Also, we were now approaching the outer wall of Canto Grande, and with each passing day there was an increasing danger that the prison guards might hear the sounds of underground digging. We were all agreed that the purchase of the truck was absolutely essential to win our battle against time.

The truck was bought "illegally" at the end of March 1990 with false identification documents because after its final task of hauling away the escapees it would have to be abandoned, and the police would certainly do their utmost to trace its ownership. Meanwhile, if Luis Angel were stopped by the police and asked to show the car papers, he could simply claim that the real owner was a cousin of his who was currently working in Arequipa. The spacious truck bed was a joy to the entire team. It easily handled all the dirt that spewed out of the tunnel mouth, and the entire team was optimistic that the digging would go twice as fast as before.

The workday lengthened to eighteen hours, but inexplicably, the expected rate of advance did not double as they had expected it to, but only increased by about fifty percent. Antonio pondered the problem and decided that it was essentially caused by the lack of incentives on the part of each team. He and Armando calculated that in order to meet the July deadline, the digging had to advance at the rate of three meters per day.

Antonio called an evaluation meeting and suggested a basic change in working methods. He proposed that the diggers be reorganized into two teams again, and that each team be held responsible for advancing the tunnel one and a half meters during its shift, no matter how long it took. Members of each team would rotate as diggers, haulers and timberers as they themselves determined, but they would keep working until they had fulfilled their daily quota.

This method won general acceptance and members of each team went to work eagerly to get the daily job done in as short a time as possible. For the first time the excavation process had been placed on an assembly line basis; the tunnel advanced at the rate of three meters per day, and the dirt flowed steadily back to the entrance despite the fact that it now took the mine car 20 minutes to cover the distance of 150 or 160 meters.

Huge rocks continued to be the major obstacle to a steady advance, and there were many days when one team had to remain below ground for six to eight hours in order to complete their quota of 1 1/2 meters. Jaime describes how it was to be working at the tunnel face:

We had to work as if we were surgeons with scalpels and other medical instruments when we ran into rocks of different sizes. We had to work cautiously, quietly, because we were now close to the prison wall, almost underneath Guard Tower No. 8 and we couldn't afford to make any noise. We had to treat the rocks tenderly, lovingly. We used different sized chisels, levers and padded hammers to coax them out of the wall one by one. The other major problem was the ventilation whenever the electricity went off. We had enough illumination with auto headlights and car batteries, but after 15 or 20 minutes the air would go dead, and we'd have to spell each other at the digging.

After experimenting with different types and sizes of mine cars, they finally settled on a model that everybody felt comfortable with. It carried between six and eight sacks of dirt, and it was light enough that it could be pushed by one man, but as the tunnel grew longer it took half an hour to 35 minutes to make the trip to the entrance in a bent over position. It was hard on the kidneys, and the transporters inevitably acquired new scratches and abrasions each day that Paloma had to clean and paint with merthiolate when they came off shift.

Jaime was the digger one day when the consistency of the dirt altered subtly. The wedge end of his crowbar sank more deeply than usual into the packed earth of the tunnel face. He pried out several more scoops of dirt and thrust his hand into the cavity. It was damp. He turned and spoke excitedly to the transporter:

"Pass the word back to Antonio: we're under the water tower."

From the vantage point of the safe house, the prison water tower was aligned directly behind Tower No. 8 and was located in the twenty-meter strip of "no-man's-land" between the prison's outer wall and the chain link fence five meters high that kept the prisoners from straying into forbidden territory. The tower guards had orders to shoot to kill anybody appearing in that free-fire zone.

The water tower leaked, and a small puddle of water accumulated beneath it before penetrating the ground. Armando had forecast that the diggers would detect dampness in the earth when the tunnel reached that point, and now Jaime had confirmed his prophecy. More important, the water tower was the single concrete point of reference the tunnelers had during their entire underground trajectory. For the first time they had solid proof that the second leg of the tunnel — now 150 meters long — had been aimed in exactly the right direction.

Luis Angel brought Armando to the safe house that night; Jaime led him the 185 meters to the tunnel face, and he corroborated for himself that the dampness could only come from the water tower. Back in the safe house, he extracted the prison plan from his attaché case and drew a line from the water tower to the rear of patios 1-A and 1-B.

"That's our next direction," he told the others, "the compass heading will be 5.13 degrees west. And what shall we name this leg?"

The diggers had already decided that.

"'Heroes and Martyrs of Los Molinos,'" they chorused. And thus the third leg of the Canto Grande tunnel got underway.

CHAPTER 15

The only MRTA prisoners inside Canto Grande who knew the tunnel project was underway could not understand why the digging went so slowly. Rodrigo described the psychological tensions that afflicted them:

A prisoner always yearns for his freedom. We on the inside felt a constant anguish at the snail-like progress that was being made, whereas the *compañeros* on the outside had a cooler, more dispassionate view of the project and a better understanding of the obstacles and security problems that were encountered and the time it took to overcome them. It's not that we didn't understand these delays, but we became more and more exasperated with the passage of time. After all, nearly three years had gone by since the inception of the plan. Also, we only had rudimentary information as to how the work was progressing outside. The visitors who passed us information couldn't go into detail. Just as one example, Ciro came to me one night and told me how he had sneaked into the "no-man's-land" between Pavilion's 1-B and 2-A and pressed his ear to the earth to see if he could hear any sounds of underground digging that would indicate the tunnelers were drawing near. I decided to break the news to him that the tunnel hadn't even passed under Tower No. 8 and penetrated into the prison compound. It nearly broke his heart.

Meanwhile, the work of mapping the underground passageways in minute detail continued. The crucial routes that had to be opened were from Pavilion 2-A to the admissions building, where the women prisoners were locked in on the floor above the clinic, and from Pavilion 2-A all the way around to Pavilion 6-B, adjoining Victor Polay's third-floor cell in the *venusterio*. Some of the locked gates and steel doors along these two subterranean passageways had proven recalcitrant and efforts to make keys for the locks had failed. A breakthrough was finally achieved when the prisoners discovered the virtues of caustic soda. When this was applied to the bolt heads atop the door hinges and the application was renewed every several days, the bolt heads slowly melted, and the entire door or gate could simply be lifted up and removed from the hinges. Facsimiles of the bolt heads were smuggled into Canto Grande and secured to the bolts with Epoxy glue.

Another important preparatory measure undertaken months in advance was the construction of an enclosed latrine in the open patio of Pavilion 2-A. It was announced that this was to be closed except on days when women visitors were allowed into the prison, as it was intended for their exclusive use. In reality, the women's latrine served a double purpose: first, it added to the impression that the MRTA prisoners were constantly improving the conditions of their living area to make their lengthy incarceration as comfortable as possible. Much more important, however, it was intended as the possible prison end of the tunnel. The entire patio of Pavilion 2-A was cemented over to discourage any tunneling attempts from the patio itself. It had always been envisioned that the tunnel would have its outlet in the patio, but due to its length and its various twists and turns, it would be a veritable miracle were it to surface at an exact predetermined point. Armando anticipated that when it reached the surface, the diggers would find themselves somewhere under the cemented floor of the patio, where it would be impossible to break through the concrete rapidly and noiselessly. Hence the need for the women's latrine, where the concrete had been perforated and the necessary escape hatch already existed. The other possible exit point lay in the triangular patch of "no-man's-land" where the fronts of Pavilions 1-B and 2-A nearly abutted. This area was fenced off but was not paved with concrete, so a tunnel exit at that point could be opened almost noiselessly.

Still another necessary preparatory measure for the escape was to make sure that all the prisoners were in tiptop physical condition and able to make the 350-meter dash for freedom in a hunched-over, crouching position without collapsing. Well before the time arrived, Rodrigo ordered the leaders of the morning exercises to make sure that everyone did fifty deep knee bends every day. The purpose, of course, was to get their leg muscles in shape for the coming ordeal.

"Forty-five, forty-six, forty-seven, forty-eight, forty-nine, and...fifty."

Victor Polay grunted as he pushed himself erect after the last knee bend and exhaled explosively. Months of sedentary prison life and excessive carbohydrates in the daily diet had girdled his midriff with extra pounds, and now the time had come to work them off. He was subjecting himself to the same physical-fitness campaign that he had prescribed for the other MRTA prisoners, and besides the setting-up exercises he performed in his cell on awakening, he jogged for an hour each morning and each afternoon in the small patio behind the *venusterio*.

He had also gradually changed his sleeping habits in preparation for the forthcoming escape. Whereas he had previously turned in with the other prisoners on the third floor after the evening television programs ended, he now went downstairs at midnight and chatted with the general until they set out the pieces on the chessboard and continued their endless nightly tournament. The general was an inveterate night owl who usually went to bed near dawn and slept through the morning. When their chess match ended at 3:30 or 4, Victor would stretch, yawn, and bid the general goodnight, then go clattering up the stairs to his own cell, taking care to make enough noise so that the Republican guard on the first floor would sleepily make a mental note that Polay was on his way up to bed as usual.

To make up for the lost hours of sleep, Victor took a substantial siesta after lunch each day. He knew that when the tunnel opened, the escape would have to take place before dawn, after the guards changed shifts at 3, and the new watch had been given enough time to grow somnolent. It was also clear to him and Rodrigo that the escape could not be scheduled after a visitors' day at Canto Grande, because the common prisoners, having received cash or food from their family, would exchange it for liquor or cocaine paste and frequently stay up celebrating all night long.

Jaime and Paloma had known each other casually before they were thrown together at close quarters, night and day for eighteen months. Paloma knew that Jaime had been involved in a relationship with another woman before he was sent to prison and then had come directly from prison to work on the tunnel.

We interviewed Paloma and Jaime separately about their participation in the project, and then — after Jaime blurted out something to the effect that the Canto Grande excavation had also turned out to be the backdrop of a budding romance — we interviewed them together late one evening in the Lima safe house.

"We felt attracted to each other from the beginning," Paloma confessed, "but it's natural to feel a warm affection for all those with whom you share dangers and difficulties. Also, I'd heard about the 'other woman,' and I was careful to behave in a neutral manner as one does when a man is committed to someone else. But still, I felt there was something supernatural at work."

"The other thing was all over. It was in the past, but Paloma wouldn't believe me," Jaime protested.

"That's because you don't have a trustworthy face," Paloma retorted.

"It all started in the house," Jaime said. "We were together all the time. Paloma had to learn her job, and I helped her as much as I could when I wasn't digging."

"I thought things over for a long time," Paloma volunteered. "I was worried that if we fell in love we wouldn't do our jobs properly, that somehow it would be an undisciplined, unrevolutionary thing to do. But at the same time, I believe one has to make a revolution happily, smiling and looking into each other's eyes, because at any moment you can die, or be captured, tortured, and sent to prison for years."

"Wasn't the problem with Jorge another complication?" Claribel asked.

"Of course. Jorge saw that we were becoming very close, and he was jealous. He declared himself to me one day, saying he had always dreamt of falling in love with a girl like me, and he begged me to please stop flirting with Jaime.

"I told him I wasn't flirting — well, not very much — but the fact is that Jaime is volatile and full of life, and I get along very well with him because he's a happy person and always bubbling over with new ideas. But Jorge started pressuring me, and I had no idea how he felt until then. I told him: 'I want to clear things up. Jaime isn't my *compañero*, but neither are you, so you have no right to dictate to me.' At that point, he said he thought we were both behaving badly and he was going to call a meeting to complain."

"That was an immature reaction on his part," Jaime broke in. "Jorge should have realized that sentimental relations are involuntary and can't be negotiated, but he was young and bullheaded, and he insisted on making a complicated, noisy issue of it."

"Was this a meeting of the whole group?" we asked.

"No, it was just Antonio and the three of us," Paloma replied, "but I wanted to sink through the floor, because Jorge accused Jaime of betraying his previous girlfriend, who was also a member of the organization, and said that Jaime's opportunistic conduct disappointed him. His words implied that I was a loose woman, and that really wounded me. Then Jaime spoke up and said the other affair was a thing of the past, and he admitted he was in love with me.

"Finally, I told them that I had come here to do a job and that was my principal objective. The party had chosen us to accomplish this task, and we were wasting time with these emotional squabbles. In the end, we all agreed that the closed environment and our own emotional immaturity were to blame for the incident, and that we should put it behind us and get on with the job."

But it wasn't easy, Paloma admitted, because they still felt strongly attracted to each other. She particularly recalled the incident of the rose.

"One day Jaime gave me a rose from the garden, and I put it in a glass of water in the kitchen. Some days later he came up from the tunnel to ask me for some medicine because his stomach was bothering him, and he saw the rose was still there. Go ahead and tell them what you told me."

Jaime was visibly embarrassed, but he replied.

"Something about how a rose that once blossomed was now withering and fading away, and how could we permit that to happen? After that our relationship kept on developing in an inevitable way."

"But how did you find a chance to talk to each other with so many people in the house?" Claribel was curious about practical details.

"We talked to each other normally in front of the others," Jaime replied, "and none of the *compañeros* knew that..."

"And besides, we'd go down to the library late at night where we could talk and read," Paloma interrupted, "because Jaime loves to read. That was our way of getting away from the others."

"The tunnel, of course!" Claribel exclaimed. "Wonderful! It turned out to be a tunnel of love as well as a freedom tunnel."

The two of them blushed and exchanged complicitous smiles.

When Paloma's back began to bother her in November 1989, Jaime helped her in the kitchen when he finished his work shift.

"I scoured pots and pans, swept and mopped, and cleaned up the kitchen," Jaime grinned. "I washed clothes and the household linen, and I peeled thousands of potatoes. By January her pain was unbearable, and we had to bring in a "cousin" to take over the job."

Paloma's sciatic nerve was affected, and she had to sleep with a board under her thin mattress. She was also in a state of deep depression, because the muscles in one of her legs were visibly atrophying, and she feared she would become paralyzed or even lose the leg.

The MRTA doctor who came to the safe house periodically to examine her, agreed that palliatives were not helping, and she would have to submit to a delicate and dangerous operation. Luis Angel drove her to the hospital and registered her, and the following day she underwent the operation. It was successful, and by the fifth day she was walking.

"While she was in the hospital, I was delegated to come to Lima and buy the big truck," Jaime said. "It took several days to find one the right size, in good condition, but not flashy enough to draw attention. Because of that, I was able to come and visit her with Luis Angel as soon as she awoke after the operation."

"I came to, and there they were," Paloma recalled. "I was deeply touched by those two wonderful people, closer than brothers, who seemed to be the only ones concerned about my condition at that moment."

Paloma left the hospital after eight days and spent the next two weeks convalescing at the home of a friend. When she returned to the operational base, she was walking normally and relieved of pain, and she gradually resumed her share of the household duties. The only limitation on her activities was a prohibition against lifting weights.

But Paloma's brush with disfigurement and paralysis had led her to think deeply about her relationship with Jaime, and she came to the conclusion that it was hypocritical to continue dissembling before the other members of the team. Jaime heartily agreed.

"When I returned, there was an evaluation session to analyze how the work was going, and Jaime and I took the opportunity to announce to everybody that we were now *compañeros*. We did that to dispel any doubts or possible misunderstandings."

"And how did the others react to the news?"

"Nobody was really surprised," Jaime said. "They had all seen it coming, and they accepted it as something natural."

"And what was Jorge's reaction?"

"He had no visible reaction. Life went on as before," Jaime recalled.

"He was finally convinced," Paloma said, "and we kept on being friends to the very end."

"That's wonderful!" Claribel exclaimed, to bring the evening session to a close.

Meanwhile, for what seemed like the first time since the inception of the project, the digging proceeded smoothly and steadily and the tunnel steadily crept forward beneath the Canto Grande prison compound at the rate of three meters a day.

Armando was able to visit the safe house more frequently during the excavation of the "Heroes and Martyrs of Los Molinos" leg and he often spent the entire night there. Armando had an obsession about tunnels, and during one of our conversations he waxed eloquent on the subject.

I was always happy to go down in the tunnel. I got used to it, and sometimes I worked down there at night. It's a bit gloomy, dark and damp, but it has a certain charm. There's nothing more amazing than total darkness. When you turn out the lights, you feel a complete solitude and absence of light. I would do this frequently and lie down, feeling a tranquil, agreeable sensation. They say it's a psychological technique using sensory deprivation that is very relaxing. I always felt calm working at night. And it's beautiful when you've been down below for a long time to come out and look up at the starry sky.

Nevertheless, Armando's mind was troubled. The tunnel now extended more than 200 meters underground and included two sharp curves, one to the left and another to the right. The fact that the diggers had hit their first objective — the water tower — squarely on the nose gave him a sense of confidence. But that had been a simple calculation, because the water tower was visible from the roof of the operational base, and he had only to calculate for the displacement created by the first, "Che Lives," leg of the tunnel. The MRTA had secured several general architectural plans of Canto Grande, each of which showed its geographical orientation with respect to due north. The problem that gnawed at his mind was that these maps disagreed with each other as to the true orientation of the prison compound, and an error of a few degrees in setting the direction of the final leg of the tunnel could lead to a mistake of twenty or thirty meters in arriving at the predetermined exit point. His only instrument for setting the course to be followed was a surveyor's theodolite, which was difficult to use in the cramped underground space, and he had no way of doubl-checking the accuracy of his calculations. The MRTA prisoners had unsuccessfully taken various compass readings from different points inside Canto Grande to try to establish the prison's orientation with respect to magnetic north, but their results contradicted each other.

I visited Canto Grande myself — he told us — and took surreptitious compass readings and made observations which led me to conclude that the plans in our possession were skewed by between fifteen and thirty degrees, which is a tremendous error. The *compañeros* inside had an ordinary, nonprofessional compass, but there is such a maze of iron reinforcing bars in the walls that the compass was thrown off and we couldn't trust the results. In the end, they took about thirty readings from different positions, and I drew up an average reading which I felt was more or less correct. We set our course inside the compound by that reading, but I knew we were flying blind and would have to make another correction before setting off on the final leg.

CHAPTER 16

I was awakened one morning by the sound of a heavy tractor motor in the outer patio — Victor recounted. — From the corridor window a narrow slice of the no-man's-land next to Tower No. 8 was visible, and there I could see a heavy caterpillar bulldozer digging a trench parallel to the wall of the outer enclosure. A prison trusty was standing next to me, watching the activity, and I asked him: "What's happening out there? Are they finally putting in a water reservoir?" "No," he said, "they're looking for a tunnel. Last night the guards in the tower heard digging noises. They think it's coming from Pavilion 6-A, and now they're trying to uncover it."

An icy hand clutched at Victor's heart. He knew, of course, that the tunnel had penetrated beneath Tower No. 8 and the water tank and was now aimed at the patio of Pavilion 2-A. One of the diggers had been careless, and the guards had heard him. The MRTA chief watched helplessly as the bulldozer relentlessly pushed sand out of the trench and slowly disappeared from sight below ground level. As he watched, a heavy steam roller chugged into the enclosure and started trundling ponderously back and forth parallel to the trench in an attempt to cave in the tunnel with its sheer weight. Later, it was joined by a third piece of heavy construction equipment: a mechanized trencher that started banging its heavy excavating shovel against the ground in the area between the bulldozed trench and Pavilion 6-A.

The occupants of 6-A were drug traffickers — Victor continued — and it was natural to think they were the tunnelers because they were closest to where the digging sounds had been heard. Besides, they were the richest group of prisoners and had the money to bribe guards and smuggle digging tools into Canto Grande. It was also natural for the authorities to assume that the tunnel originated under Pavilion 6-A and was heading toward the outer wall. It never occurred to them that the tunnel originated outside the walls and was aimed inward. And it never crossed their minds that the MRTA could be digging a tunnel, because our group was on the fourth floor of Pavilion 2-A, and the lower floors were occupied by common prisoners, with a generous sprinkling of stool pigeons. An excavation could never be hidden from them.

Inside the tunnel itself, the diggers were first paralyzed by the sounds of the bulldozer's engine and its clanking treads passing back and forth overhead, and then by the dull, booming explosions every time the trenching tractor banged its shovel against the earth.

"They've found us." Jaime was desperate as another thud freed a shower of sand particles above his head. He and Armando were at the tunnel face where the overhead had not yet been stuccoed with cement gruel. Armando, his jaw clenched with anxiety, listened to the noises above that carried clearly through the earth.

"They've heard us," he corrected Jaime, "but they haven't found us yet. Stop the digging, and let's get back to the base."

One of the diggers was posted at the turn where the second leg of the tunnel merged into the new "Heroes and Martyrs of Los Molinos" leg. His task was to report to the safe house if any cave-ins occurred. Armando and Jaime scurried the length of the tunnel and climbed the vertical ladder. Paloma and her "cousin" María busied themselves outside the house as lookouts in case a guard patrol started making a house-to-house search of the neighborhood, while the entire team busied themselves inside to remove all evidence that the base was occupied by eighteen people rather than four. Bedrolls, sleeping bags, changes of clothing, as well as extra plates and cutlery were stowed in the underground library and the cover of the tunnel shaft was poised for instant lowering as soon as the last digger disappeared into the earth in the event of a police raid.

Armando sat at the dining-room table and reviewed the situation. During the past week, the underground terrain through which the tunnel was advancing had changed from a compact sand and dirt mixture with only occasional large rocks, to a difficult, boulder-studded composition of soil. Undoubtedly, one of the diggers had banged the wedge end of his crowbar into a boulder and the sound had carried up to the surface. What was done was done and couldn't be corrected now, but Armando felt confident that the tunnel could not be uncovered by overhead trenching because, according to his calculations, it was at least fifteen meters below the surface, and no bulldozer could dig that deep without caving in the sides of the trench.

Canto Grande is located at the upper edge of an alluvial plain that slopes imperceptibly downward to the plain of Lima from the first escarpments of the Andean foothills. To the naked eye, the terrain appears level, but Armando's calculations with the theodolite informed him that the ground level of the Canto Grande compound was at least nine meters higher than ground level at the safe house, and he had made sure that the tunnel kept to a dead-level horizontal course despite its twists and turns. This ensured that by the time the diggers penetrated beneath the outer wall of the prison they would be at least fifteen meters below the surface. Armando closed his eyes and imaginatively placed himself inside the mind of any Canto Grande prison official. It was against all logic and inconceivable to the prison mentality that would-be escapees should dig straight down for fifteen meters before leveling off to a horizontal course and heading for the nearest outer wall. If they dug down fifteen meters — and where would they hide all that dirt? — they would have to dig upward the same distance to get back to the surface when the tunnel reached a safe exit point. And where, to reiterate, would the tunnelers hide all that dirt? No, Armando shook his head. He was confident that the tunnel was safe from discovery.

Victor Polay tells of his reaction to the suddenly increased tension:

It took us two days to get word to the safe house about what was happening inside the prison, but of course they already knew from the sounds of the bulldozer and trencher overhead, and they had suspended digging. It was during that time that the new prison commandant visited the *venusterio* and spoke to Victor.

"What do you think we're doing out there, *Señor* Polay?" he asked me.

"I imagine you're putting in a water reservoir," I said.

"No," he told me, "we're hunting for a tunnel that the narcos are digging."

"If you're so worried about tunnels," I suggested, "why don't you dig a moat five meters deep running all the way around the outer wall?"

"You know, that's not such a bad idea," he said thoughtfully.

Actually, every prison official always suffers from tunnel psychosis. While I was in Canto Grande they discovered two tunnels being dug by common prisoners, not to mention the first tunnel the MRTA tried to dig. And the current flurry of activity deepened that psychosis.

I remember one day I was in the *venusterio* patio talking to Major Jara and Captain Castillo, and Major Jara said:

"You aren't looking well, Mr. Polay; you're losing weight. What's wrong? Aren't your *compañeros* feeding you properly?"

"No," I replied. "I'm dieting to lose weight so I can escape through your tunnel over there."

They nearly died laughing.

"It's true," I went on. "I read about the tunnel escape in Chile several years ago, and there was a fat man who got stuck halfway through. He deserved it, of course, but the worst part was that all the prisoners behind him were prevented from completing their escape. So I'm taking no chances."

They all thought that was terribly funny, and it never entered their minds that it might be true. After all, they knew that I was counting on negotiating an amnesty with Vargas Llosa after the elections. And here I was, cooped up with captains, majors, colonels, and generals in the maximum-security ward. There was more army brass around me than if I'd been imprisoned in a military fortress.

The bulldozer dug a trench five meters deep and some twenty-five meters long in two days, while the steam roller and trencher moved ponderously back and forth over the area where the digging noises had been heard. Their efforts were in vain, and, to Victor's immense relief, on the third day they were withdrawn. Republican guards continued hammering iron probes into the soil, but to no avail. Armando's calculations had been vindicated, and the tunnel kept on advancing at a depth of fifteen meters.

The patch of rocky soil cleared up, almost miraculously, and the diggers now found themselves penetrating into an area of hard, compacted sand that was ideal for excavation. The tunnel walls and overhead were so firm that timbering was unnecessary and only the overhead was stuccoed. Despite the precautions taken to work silently, the two shifts were now progressing steadily at the rate of three meters per day, and the eighty meters of the "Heroes and Martyrs of Los Molinos" leg was completed in four weeks.

It was now the beginning of June 1990, and the deadline for completion imposed by the National Directorate was only six weeks away. Three new arrivals joined the team to make a total of eighteen diggers, plus four above ground in the household staff, or a total of twenty-two people crowded into the cramped safe house. Through months of close-quarters living and hard-won experience underground, the entire team now functioned like a well-oiled machine. The dirt moved steadily back from the tunnel face in three one-man carts, was hoisted to the surface and hauled away in the truck. Huge amounts of high-calorie food arrived regularly to be prepared by Paloma and María and dispensed to the hungry crew.

Armando calculated that the tunnel had reached the rear corner of the patio belonging to Pavilion 1-A and a course correction was now required to steer it beneath Patios 1-A and 1-B and into the patio area of Pavilion 2-A. Leg No. 4 — a short stretch of only thirteen meters — veered to the left and was christened, *Hasta la victoria siempre*, (Until victory, always) from a celebrated phrase by Che Guevara. It was made necessary to avoid digging beneath the two pavilions themselves. This leg was accomplished in five days, and Armando set the final course to bring the tunnel beneath the patio of 2-A to its exit point in the no-man's-land beside the MRTA pavilion.

With the new *compañeros*, we now had two shifts of nine workers in each team — Antonio recalls — but the digging conditions continued to be difficult. When the electricity went off there was no ventilation, only emergency lighting, and the heat was always stifling. Under those conditions we discovered that we could make the best progress by working twenty-four hours a day, including Sundays, and dividing the team into two shifts of twelve hours each. That way, each team got twelve hours or more of rest after completing its quota, and everyone was fresh and motivated when they started work again. We also decided we could reduce the dimensions of the tunnel on the last leg to one meter high by seventy centimeters wide, and this enabled us to start progressing at the rate of five meters a day.

The final stretch was christened *Tupac Amaru, libertador* (Tupac Amaru, liberator), and Armando estimated its length at somewhere between sixty and seventy-five meters. Halfway through its excavation he instructed the diggers to start sloping the tunnel toward the surface at the rate of one meter's rise for each three meters advanced.

June drew to an end, and the digging slowed as the tunnel penetrated another patch of almost cement-like sand. It was also made more difficult because the mine cars were unusable on the upward slope, and the dirt-filled sacks had to be hauled down to level ground before being loaded into the carts.

Antonio was digging at the tunnel face late one afternoon when he dropped his crowbar and pressed his ear to the sandy wall.

"Ricardito," he called to one of the haulers, "go get Armando and tell him to bring his stethoscope. I can hear the *bombo*."

CHAPTER 17

The MRTA musical group in Canto Grande had achieved professional quality after practicing together daily over a period of nearly two years. The instruments were a motley collection: two guitars, two *quenas* (the bamboo Andean shepherd's flute), a *charanga* or five-string soprano guitar, various percussion instruments, and a large *bombo* drum whose deep throbbing tone set the beat for the musicians and the choral group.

Initially, they had practiced in the corridor of the fourth floor of their pavilion, preparing concerts which they presented in the patio on visitors' days. During the past few months, however, on instructions passed along from Armando, they had started giving daily concerts in the patio for the entertainment of all the prison inmates. The musicians and the twelve-man choral group assembled along the wall that separated the patio from the triangular patch of no-man's-land and started playing and singing punctually at 5 p.m. The *bombo* drum rested on the cement floor of the patio, and its deep bass note reverberated through the earth, providing a subterranean sonar beacon to guide the tunnelers to their final exit point.

Armando pressed past Antonio and applied his stethoscope to different points at the face and sides of the tunnel.

"I can even hear the guitars and the voices," he told Antonio. "They're singing the MRTA hymn. They are right on schedule, and we are right on course."

There were other surface noises that carried down to the tunnel. The world soccer championship play-offs were underway in Italy, and prisoners and guards alike clustered around every television set in Canto Grande. Because of the frequent blackouts, the Republican guards had brought a gasoline generator into the central patio so they could follow the matches even when the power failed. During these periods, the throbbing of the gasoline motor provided another directional point of reference for the diggers.

Armando planned to bring the tunnel to the surface under the patio of Pavilion 2-A and he expected to find himself somewhere beneath the concrete paving which covered the entire patio. Then, using the paving as the tunnel overhead, he intended to dig horizontally from that point either toward the ready-made exit of the women's latrine or toward the natural dirt surface of the no-man's-land between Pavilion 1-B and 2-A, whichever was closer.

The next two days were spent probing upward at a thirty-degree angle, and Armando approved a reduction in the dimensions to a square excavation measuring seventy by seventy centimeters. On the third day, the diggers discovered to their dismay that the hard, compacted sand they had been tunneling through was gradually giving way to a looser mixture of sand and earth that came showering down every time they raked the overhead with their crowbars. Jaime called Armando to the tunnel face and demonstrated the problem to him.

"This is the most dangerous terrain we've struck so far," he worried. "We could have a cave-in at any minute. Don't you think we should start timbering again?"

Armando inspected the overhead carefully with his flashlight.

"We should have anticipated this," he said thoughtfully. "We're very close to the surface now, and we're running into the loose earth fill that was bulldozed when the prison was under construction. The tunnel is too small and the slope is too steep for timbering, so we'll have to keep tunneling upward and hope for the best."

The earth around them was now a mixture of dirt and sand that had not been compacted by centuries of rain and compression. The digger at the tunnel face was ordered to tie a rope around his waist as a safety precaution, so that in case of a cave-in his companions could pull him out by brute force before he smothered.

It was Sunday, a visitors' day and the final day of the world football championship. Digging was proceeding around the clock, and Antonio's group came on duty at 4 p.m.

The leader of the previous team warned me that the earth was soft and no longer sandy — he told us. — There was also a shortage of sacks by then because many of them had been torn on protruding rocks now that the tunnel dimensions were so much smaller. When I reached the tunnel face I found the situation really frightening. All I had to do was scratch the overhead and the earth came showering down. The worst of it was that we estimated we were still at least eight meters underground, and that's a lot of dirt hanging over one's head. We also had the fixed idea that we were going to come up under the concrete layer of the patio floor and would have to tunnel horizontally from there.

I happened to be the one who was digging when it happened. The noise above me was louder than ever, and I even thought I could hear footsteps, when suddenly the earth caved in over my head. I threw myself backward into the tunnel so I wouldn't be buried. But strangely enough, the quantity of earth that came down wasn't very great, and when it stopped I inched forward and found myself looking up at a dim round light. I couldn't see very well, and at first I didn't understand what had happened. I shone my flashlight upward, then turned it off, and I began to realize

I was looking up at the sky. It was 6:30, twilight time, and the light was dim. I could hear the murmur of voices overhead, but it wasn't until a current of fresh air began to flow against my face that it suddenly dawned on me that we'd finally reached our goal: the Canto Grande tunnel was open from end to end.

CHAPTER 18

Two "pelicans" were lounging with their backs against the wall that separated the trash-strewn no-man's-land from the patios of pavilions 1-B and 2-A. It was Sunday evening and the day's visitors had departed. The uncle of one of them had pressed a few bills into the hands of his nephew before leaving, and the latter had immediately invested his windfall in several joints of cocaine paste. Now they were dreamily passing one of the hand-rolled cigarettes back and forth between them, drawing the smoke deep into their lungs.

The pelicans are the poorest of the poor among Canto Grande's common prisoners and consequently the most diligent and cunning thieves. Either they have no family outside to keep them supplied with food and other amenities, or their families have given up hope of rehabilitating them and only visit them sporadically as a Christian obligation.

Cocaine paste is the result of the first step of reducing Andean coca leaves to refined cocaine. The dried leaves are stuffed into a fifty-gallon drum at the plantation where they are harvested, a mixture of sulfuric acid and kerosene is poured over them, and they are mashed by hand with heavy wooden mortars until they give off their alkaloid content. The poisonous liquid is strained off, leaving a thick paste: the product that is shipped to the refining laboratories of the Medellín drug cartel in Colombia. Cocaine paste mixed with tobacco is readily obtainable in Peru. It is cheap, because it rots the brain and rapidly reduces the smoker to a shambling vestige of humanity. Its use in the Canto Grande penitentiary was tacitly encouraged by prison authorities as a nonviolent means of keeping their wards stupefied and controllable. It had the additional benefit of providing a welcome source of extra income to the ill-paid Republican guards and prison employees.

The generous host of this private party utilized a roach-clip to finish the joint, snuffed it out, and got up heavily to urinate. Out of deference to the other, he started crossing the earthen area to the opposite wall when, abruptly, he staggered and one leg disappeared into the ground up to his hip.

His startled companion helped extricate him, and both of them stared down into the hole that had magically appeared. A flashlight beam shone up at them and then clicked off.

"Son-of-a-bitch!" the first breathed. "It's a goddamn tunnel!"

"Yeah!" the other agreed, "and it's gotta be the MRTA gang next door that's digging it."

The first stripped off his jacket and spread it over the hole.

"We better go find Pichirulo," he decided. "He'll know how to handle this."

I was on guard duty that Sunday — Ciro recalled when the MRTA delegate came hurrying up to me and said:

"Two of the common prisoners claim they have discovered a tunnel in no-man's-land."

I didn't know what the exact situation was, but I went immediately to inform Rodrigo, and on the way I alerted all the others on the fourth floor and told them to get ready to leave. I left them with their mouths hanging open.

Rodrigo sent me downstairs to find out what was happening, and I found Pichirulo waiting for me. He was more or less the straw boss of the common prisoners in the patio, and we were on good terms with each other. We ducked through the small metal door that led to no-man's-land and Pichirulo picked up a jacket lying on the ground. The hole underneath it was small, only about a foot in diameter, and the two prisoners who had discovered it were standing there. I admitted to the three of them that they had discovered our tunnel and warned them they had to keep quiet about it until we could patch up the hole.

Naturally, they assumed we were digging our way out of the prison, from Pavilion 2-A toward the wall. I told them they would be well rewarded for keeping their mouths shut, and I gave them some money to buy liquor, cigarettes, cocaine paste, whatever. All three of them, including Pichirulo, were convinced they'd struck gold and were already looking forward to months of blackmailing the organization in return for their silence while we dug our way out of Canto Grande.

I realized that the *compañeros* down below in the tunnel were probably as shocked and confused as I was and had no idea what was happening overhead, so I knelt down, put my mouth to the hole and called down:

"*Patria o muerte!*"

Back came the countersign, "*Venceremos!*" They knew then that we had control of the exit, and I told them to bring us weapons. The man below replied that they were already on the way, and I began to breathe more easily.

Ciro replaced the jacket over the hole and ordered the two discoverers to remain where they were. He hastened to the MRTA quarters on the ground floor of 2-A, alerted Pedro, the squad chief, as to what had happened and sent the latter and his team of four to no-man's-land to keep an eye on the two discoverers and to receive the consignment of weapons when it arrived. He left Pichirulo in their charge and returned to the fourth floor to report to Rodrigo.

Nobody had expected the tunnel to be opened until at least the coming Tuesday, and its premature discovery by three common prisoners had all the earmarks of an impending disaster.

My father and I had been talking until 5, when he left with the rest of the visitors — Rodrigo recalled — and I was resting on my bunk in the empty cell when Ciro came rushing in, shouting, "Rodrigo, we're leaving, we're leaving!"

I sat up, bumping my head on the upper bunk, and asked: "What's going on?"

"The commons have found the tunnel!" He was on the verge of having a heart attack. "We've got to get everyone ready to move out."

I sent him downstairs to find out exactly what had happened, and I sat there for a few moments, trying to organize my thoughts. We had known the tunnel was almost finished, and we of the Internal Directorate had been ready for weeks. Just a few days before, we had gone over the final plans for the escape, rechecking what each of the special teams had to do and what their plans were in case anything went wrong. The National Directorate had discarded this Sunday as D-day because it was a visitors' day and besides the final match of the world soccer championship had ended a few hours before with Germany's victory over Argentina, and everyone was staying up late to watch the replay. We expected the tunnel to open on Tuesday or Thursday, and those of us in the know were coordinating our plans to make the break early the following morning.

The most urgent priority was to establish communications links with the safe-house base, the women prisoners in admissions, and with *Comandante* Polay in the *venusterio*. Margarita had smuggled three walkie-talkies into the prison several weeks previously, and for the past two days I had maintained an open line with the safe house. I picked up my handset, and Paloma answered my call. She didn't know the tunnel was open. Of course! It was a long three blocks of hard going, and the news hadn't reached her yet. As I was talking to her, Antonio popped up out of the entrance shaft and took over the phone to explain what had happened inside the tunnel. I asked him how many weapons were available at the base. He replied that there were three FAL combat rifles, about ten pistols, and several hand grenades. I told him to keep one FAL and two pistols at the exit point and to pass the remainder up to us. He agreed, and I asked him about getaway vehicles. He replied that *Señor* Aldana had borrowed Luis Angel and the truck a few hours before to accomplish an errand and he didn't expect them back before 9 o'clock. As for the Dodge, it had been parked in the garage of a collaborator ever since the big truck went into service, but it could be picked up within half an hour or so.

I groaned. We were utterly dependent on the big truck and the pickup to make our escape. Armando came on the line then, and I told him to evacuate all unnecessary personnel from the safe house immediately, to get in touch with someone from the National Directorate, and to start organizing the necessary transport and activating the safe-house network for the impending influx of escapees.

By the time I finished talking, Ciro was back with his report that Pedro's team was controlling the exit and waiting for arms. Since Ciro was operations chief for coordinating the entire escape, he had dozens of things demanding his attention. Providentially, it was now dinner time, so I gave Pablo the two extra walkie-talkies which he concealed in his inside jacket pockets and told him to go pick up *Comandante* Rolando's dinner from the women's quarters and deliver it to him in the *venusterio* as usual. Then I went out to check with Pedro's Team A, Pancho's Team B, and Ernesto's contention squad, to make sure everybody was alert and ready to go.

Pablo strolled calmly into the admissions squad room and announced he had come to pick up the *comandante's* dinner. None of the Republicans paid attention to him; they were all glued to the TV set, glumly watching the defeat of the Argentine soccer team. He passed the walkie-talkie through the small window to Valentina, the chief of the women's section, and rapidly explained the situation to her. From the second floor of admissions, the women prisoners could use a pocket mirror to keep the Republican guard barracks outside the prison compound under surveillance. They were to maintain a constant watch, and if they detected any unusual activity or mobilization of guards, they were to report it to Rodrigo. That would be the signal to activate the escape plan immediately. Otherwise, they were to make their preparations for evacuation according to the pre-established plan and await further orders.

Pablo walked down the stairs with Victor Polay's dinner tray and made his way to the *venusterio* where the guards on the ground floor, also intent on the replay of the championship match, opened the grilled door and waved him upstairs.

Pablo brought me dinner that day rather than Ciro — Victor recalled. He walked in, set the tray down, and pulled a walkie-talkie out of his inside pocket.

"Here's your radio, *Comandante*," he announced. "You should get in touch with Rodrigo immediately, because some common prisoners have discovered the tunnel."

I was disconcerted, because in the first place Pablo wasn't supposed to know anything about the tunnel, and here he was, handing me a walkie-talkie, which was one of our most closely guarded secrets. I knew Rodrigo had the radios in his possession but couldn't risk passing me one until the final minutes, because the *venusterio* stool pigeons searched my cell from end to end at least twice a week. In the second place, almost anything I said would confirm the existence of the tunnel, and I couldn't chance that at this point, so I simply told him, "Thanks, that's fine," and sent him on his way.

I couldn't imagine what had happened, and I even speculated that perhaps the common prisoners were digging another tunnel that had collided with ours. I inserted the batteries and got on the circuit to Rodrigo.

He corroborated that the tunnel had opened up in no-man's-land but that the guards hadn't yet discovered it.

"What shall we do?" he asked me. "Shall we start pushing our people through the tunnel now? Shall we take over the prison militarily as soon as the weapons arrive, or shall we follow the original plan and wait until 3:30 tomorrow morning?"

I asked him what transport was available at the base, and when he answered, "None," I made up my mind.

"First of all, we have to control the people who found the tunnel and all the common prisoners in 2-A so they don't suspect what's up. Have all three teams ready to go, but let's try to hold out until tomorrow morning as planned. It's important that we all get away cleanly."

You have to understand that, from a transportation standpoint, Canto Grande is like the wide end of a funnel with the Andes forming a natural barrier to the east. The funnel narrows down towards Lima, and if there were any hullabaloo connected with our escape, it would be the easiest thing in the world for Peruvian police to throw a roadblock across the spout and pick us all up as we tried to leave the area. I wanted us to disappear quietly through the tunnel and spread out to the various safe houses awaiting us before the prison guards even realized we were gone.

Rodrigo and I were using a prearranged code so we didn't have to mention such things as weapons, tunnels, or getaway vehicles, and we employed double talk and kept our interventions to a minimum. When we finished our exchange, I realized we were on a four-way hookup, because

Valentina chimed in to say her girls were ready and there was no unusual activity at the guard barracks.

Next, Antonio came on the circuit from the safe house, and we recognized each other's voices because I had handled him directly several years earlier before I went up to the hills. It was a real pleasure to exchange greetings after all that time, and he briefed me about the transportation problem and the fact that they had so far been unable to contact anyone from the National Directorate on this Sunday evening. He promised to report back when the big truck arrived and keep us informed of any other developments. We all signed off and settled down for a long tense night of waiting.

Armando, who had spent the final three days in the safe house supervising every step of the excavation as the diggers worked their way up to the surface, felt an overwhelming surge of relief when he learned the tunnel was open in no-man's-land. He had ordered the diggers to start curving upward a bit later than he should have, with the consequence that the tunnel opened inside the earthen triangle itself rather than under the concrete "roof" of the patio. But, no matter, the hole was open in exactly the right spot and ready to receive the forty-eight fugitives in a matter of hours.

But now, at the safe-house end, the matters of transport and disposal of the escapees were the urgent priorities. The tunnel had opened accidentally and several days prematurely. While plans had been laid to activate the escape the coming Tuesday or Thursday, nobody had anticipated having to do so on Sunday night, and Armando was now the man with the monkey on his back. He, and nobody else, had to solve the problem.

There were no vehicles at the safe house — Armando recalls — and the truck wasn't due back for several hours.

Comandante Rolando (Victor Polay) asked me to get in touch with somebody in the National Directorate, but I knew this was almost impossible to accomplish on a Sunday evening. We also had to evacuate all nonessential personnel from the safe house so as to minimize casualties in the event of a shootout. We urgently needed more weapons inside the prison itself in case the breakout was discovered before everybody was cleanly away.

By now it was 8 p.m. Without quite knowing how I was going to accomplish it, I guaranteed Rolando that within two hours I would have transport available and a safe house ready to receive the escapees. I left on foot with Paloma and her "cousin" María, and we had to walk about five blocks before we could hail a taxi. We went to the home of an intermediary who knew where the old pickup was kept, and he took us there in his car. I got on the phone and tried unsuccessfully to get in touch with somebody from the National Directorate and then called a *compañera* and told her to get her house ready to receive about four dozen people.

The girls insisted on coming back to the safe house with me in case they could be of help, and on the way back we ran into a police roadblock. They were checking licenses and identity documents. María had a nervous attack at this point. She rolled down the window and started vomiting. I used that as an excuse to tell the policeman that she was sick, I gave him some money, and we got away without having to show our documents. I tried to contact the safe house with my walkie-talkie, only to discover that the battery was dead, so I drove back and left the pickup there.

The intermediary who had enabled Armando to locate the pickup truck had followed the latter back to the operational base in his own car. Luis Angel and the big truck still had not returned from their lengthy errand, and the fifteen superfluous diggers who were supposed to evacuate the safe house had to await its arrival before they could leave.

The acquisition of more arms to smuggle into the prison was an urgent priority, and one of the diggers who had arrived most recently revealed that he knew another militant who controlled an MRTA arms cache. He and Armando immediately set off in the extra car to obtain these weapons.

We arrived at the *compañero's* house — Armando said — and he agreed that, yes, he knew where the arms were buried but he needed authorization from the National Directorate to turn them over to us. It was a maddening situation. I told him I had tried unsuccessfully to contact somebody from the Directorate, and we needed the weapons urgently for an operation that was to take place before dawn. He knew that an important operation of some sort was scheduled for the next few days, and we finally talked him into releasing the arms to us. He accompanied us to the place where they were buried and helped us dig them up and load them into the car. Then we drove the *compañero* back to his home and returned to the vicinity of the operational base. Since it was too risky to drive a strange car loaded with weapons up to the door, I parked the car a few blocks away and left the other man guarding the weapons while I walked to the safe house.

I learned, to my immense relief, that during my absence the big truck had finally returned, and now it was gone again to take the extra diggers to a thoroughfare where buses were running. Since they all had legal identity documents, they would have no trouble dispersing to residences throughout the city.

The truck came back in about fifteen minutes and I had Luis Angel drive me to where the other car was waiting. It was parked in front of a vacant lot, but as we were transferring the weapons into the truck, a neighbor came out from a house across the street and watched us loading these strange packages into the truck. Fortunately, he got bored within a few minutes and went back into the house.

Luis Angel drove the truck back into the safe-house patio, while the other man and I drove to another nearby spot and left the car there, since it was to serve as one of the three getaway vehicles. Inside the safe house, they started passing weapons through the tunnel to Teams A and B and the contention squad. We soon had enough guns and grenades inside Canto Grande to control any conceivable situation militarily, and we all began to breathe more easily. By now it was after midnight, and all we had to do was wait for the prison guards to change shifts at 3 p.m. and settle down before the people inside started the escape operation.

Jaime and Jorge were below ground at the tunnel mouth, on guard against any intrusion. Jaime, clad only in briefs and tennis shoes, was armed with a Smith & Wesson .38 calibre revolver and had a walkie-talkie as well. They had passed the first consignment of arms up to Pedro's team A in no-man's-land, and after a wait of several hours they passed up the remaining weapons in the jute sacks normally used for hauling dirt. The sacks, scraping against the sides of the exit hole, enlarged it so that by now it could accommodate a human body. Since the operation was to take place in pitch darkness, orders were passed that weapons were to remain uncocked with the safety catches on. Both men had been awake for nearly twenty-four hours, but the adrenalin circulating through their systems kept them at a high pitch of alertness. The minutes ticked past in slow motion, and Jaime, who had no watch, lost all notion of passing time.

It was past midnight on the fourth floor when the Professor approached Rodrigo diffidently and said:

"You know, I've been thinking this thing over, and I've decided I'd better stay behind when you people leave."

Rodrigo was dumdfounded.

"Why on earth do you want to stay in prison?" he asked.

The Professor was the man whose arrest just before Christmas the previous year had led to the detention and incarceration of Uncle Felix. There were no specific charges against either of them: only the notation, "Suspected subversive," in the police index files.

Now, facing Rodrigo, the tubby little Professor ran his fingers through his thinning gray hair.

"Well, I'm not nearly as young as I used to be, probably the oldest man in the organization. Besides, I'm fat and asthmatic, and I have arthritis. As you know, I've skipped the hour of exercises you kids do every morning, and I'm just about sure I couldn't make it through that tunnel of yours. It has to be a long, long stretch of running bent over. No, Rodrigo, I know I'd collapse halfway there, and I don't want to spoil your chances. Even if I did make it, I'd have to go underground and spend the rest of my days as a clandestine fugitive from justice. I'm too old for that sort of existence, and I'd be a burden on the organization rather than a help."

Rodrigo looked at the old man compassionately and slowly nodded.

"You're right, Pops. Actually, I'd assigned two of the boys to pull you through if you did collapse. But you've made the right decision, and the organization is grateful that you're willing to make this sacrifice. But what are you going to do when the authorities discover that you're the only MRTA member who stayed behind? They're going to hold your feet to the fire, you know."

"I've thought of that," the Professor agreed, "and I think I'll slip over to Pavilion 1-B. I've a friend there I play chess with now and then, and he'll cover up for me until the heat is off."

So it was settled, and the old man and the young one embraced each other.

Pichirulo, who had been lounging on a nearby bench listening to their conversation, stood up, stretched, and approached Rodrigo.

"How about letting me take the Prof's place?" he suggested with ill-concealed eagerness. "After all, I've done your people lots of favors, and the biggest one I ever did was just a few hours ago."

Rodrigo grinned at the man's cheekiness but gave thought to his argument. He knew the two drug addicts who had put their feet in the MRTA tunnel were snoring heavily, stoned to the eyeballs, in a corner of no-man's-land under the watchful eyes of Ernesto's team. Pichirulo's quick thinking had undoubtedly saved the entire tunnel project from disaster at the last moment. He knew that Victor Polay, for security reasons, had limited the number of escapees to the MRTA militants in Canto Grande.

"What are you in for, Pichirulo?" he asked, "and how much time do you still have to serve?"

"Armed robbery," the other answered promptly. "Third offense, and I have eighteen years, four months and twenty-one days to go."

"All right," Rodrigo made up his mind. "It's a deal; you'll go with us."

The two men shook hands on it, and Pichirulo strutted back to his bench, beaming.

Ciro and Rodrigo, from the fourth floor balcony, observed the changing of the guard at 3 a.m., waited until the new shift in the rotunda had settled down, and then alerted the first group of twenty men to prepare for evacuation. Ernesto's contention group took up positions on the ground floor and in the patio to prevent any common prisoners from interfering with the escape.

Promptly at 3:30, Rodrigo went on the air to announce laconically,

"The first shipment is on its way."

The rotunda guard who should have been facing Pavilion 2-A had his back turned, absorbed in a newspaper, and Ciro waved the twenty men down the outside stairway in single file. They entered the work area on the ground floor and, one by one, climbed up on a bench and slipped through an oblong window that had been propped open in preparation. One after another they sat down on the ground with their feet dangling into the hole, and when Jaime called up, "Next," slid down the almost vertical shaft to land in the soft dirt at the bottom.

Jorge and I started receiving them. We had carved steps leading upward, but after the first four or five landed the hole looked more like a steep toboggan slide leading into the tunnel proper. The lights were on throughout the tunnel, and I recognized many of the first group of twenty; after all, I'd shared cells with them in Canto Grande. I'd clap them on the shoulder and shove them on their way. Uncle Felix was the seventh or eighth man out, and I gave him a special bearhug. He looked down the small, unpropped final leg of the tunnel and shook his head disapprovingly. He'd always insisted on good workmanship. We had one *compañero* stationed at the final curve, which was the hardest going, another to guide the *compañeros* through the mid-section, and a third in the library at the end to point out the vertical ladder leading up to the safe house and freedom. The first group had all made it upstairs before 4 o'clock.

As soon as the twentieth man was down the hole, Rodrigo got on the walkie-talkie again to *Comandante* Rolando.

"Alpha is coming your way," he said. "Over."

"Roger and out," Victor Polay responded.

Pedro and his group of four had trained intensively for three months to accomplish the delicate task of helping the MRTA leader escape from the third floor of the *venusterio*. Now, clad in black and wearing tennis shoes, Team A entered the subterranean corridor below the inner patio, opened the manhole cover leading to the sewage canal and made their way in pitch darkness all the way around the prison rotunda to Pavilion 6-B.

I knew that the key to success of the entire escape plan lay in getting *Comandante* Rolando out of the *venusterio* in complete silence without anyone being aware of what was happening — Pedro told us — and this was what we had trained and planned for during the past three months.

I knew my way through the sewage canal blindfolded since I had worked with Ciro on opening the doors and grills that barred our way. In our practice exercises we had reached the point where we could make it around to 6-B in fifteen minutes, and that was the time the *comandante* was counting on after receiving the message that we were coming. But that morning something happened that we hadn't counted on: a whole group of guards had gathered in front of the pavilion where we had to climb the outside stairs to the top floor, and we would be in plain view between the first and second floors. One of the guards was very close to us, but as luck would have it, four of them were sound asleep and the other two had their backs turned.

I left two of my team guarding the entrance with a revolver and combat rifle, while the rest of us awaited our chance to slip up to the second floor, one by one, while the guard facing us was distracted. That took us an extra five minutes, but it was absolutely necessary. Had he spotted us, the entire operation would have collapsed.

After Pedro and his two assistants reached the second floor, the ascent was rapid, and the three of them came out on the roof of 6-B. Pedro peered down at the rotunda to make sure no guards were watching, then stood up and clasped his hands over his head: the signal that his team was ready for the rescue.

Pedro had a rope coiled around his waist. It was improvised from several bedsheets braided in strips and dyed black. It had knots tied in it at regular intervals to give Polay handholds as he climbed. Now he uncoiled it and tossed one end down to where the bottom of the ramp joined the *venusterio* roof.

That was the longest eight hours of my life — Victor recalls — and the last five minutes went the slowest. Pedro's team was supposed to be in place fifteen minutes after I received the first signal, but the time ticked by and nothing happened. I imagined the worst, of course: that something had gone wrong, that they had been intercepted. But finally, after twenty minutes, I received the message from Rodrigo: "A is waiting for you."

I had rehearsed my escape many times in my mind, and now the actuality seemed incredibly simple. I had the keys to the first and second barred doors, and I took the chair from my cell with me. I had previously loosened the mortar around the skylight padlock with a screwdriver, and now I simply climbed up on the chair, pried out the hasp, and pushed the skylight open. I pulled myself up on the roof and started crawling across it toward the ramp leading to 6-B. This was the most dangerous stretch, since I was in full view of the guards in the rotunda and the guards in Tower No. 8, but I had dressed in black for the occasion and was nearly invisible. The rope was waiting for me, and I knotted it around my waist. I climbed hand over hand up the rope, and the *compañeros* helped pull me up the 4-meter ramp to the roof of 6-B. Ciro and Rodrigo were watching us from the fourth floor of 2-A as we disappeared down the stairway.

The last two flights were tricky going because of the guards lounging in the central patio. Most of them had their backs to us, but two of them were facing in our direction, and we had to cling to the shadows and slip across the lighted area one by one. Then we squeezed through a grilled door in which one of the lower bars had been sawed away and went down into the ducts where we were in total darkness. There were six of us now, each gripping the shoulder of the man ahead of him. I was directly behind Pedro, the leader, who knew the route by heart. He had a flashlight but didn't use it because there were other barred doors leading up to the other pavilions. The door to 2-A was open, and we climbed the internal stairway to the fourth floor.

I was wearing a scarf and a cap to avoid recognition in case we were seen on the way, and now I found myself surrounded by *compañeros* I had never met, and who didn't know me either. The organization had grown a great deal while I was in the mountains and then in prison. I embraced all of them happily, and we started downstairs with the armed protection group on all sides of me. On the ground floor we passed through a group of common prisoners who pretended to be asleep but who, in reality, were watching every move we made and who were being watched in turn by Ernesto's contention group. We went through the mess hall window, and there was the freedom tunnel a rabbit hole about one meter in diameter. What a wonderful sensation!

One *compañero* entered ahead of me, and I slid behind him down the steep slope. As I went past, a *compa* with a walkie-talkie reported to the base: "The *comandante* is on his way." One of the diggers led the way, guiding us through the tunnel. The rest of us followed him, running crouched over.

We were ten to fifteen meters underground; the air was suffocating and the heat terrible. I was wearing a cap and scarf, but when they fell off I disobeyed the primordial guerrilla injunction never to leave anything behind. The tunnel curved and then curved again, and despite the fact that I was scuttling along, hunched over, drenched with perspiration, I admired the construction work. It was a superb engineering project, and I found myself thinking of the time and effort and personal sacrifice that had gone into it.

It took us at least ten minutes to reach the end, climb the vertical ladder set into the wall and find ourselves in the base. After a hasty round of greetings, Rodrigo, Ciro, one other member of the National Directorate and I took off in a passenger car, transferred to another car at a prearranged point, and went directly to a safe house that was waiting for us. At long last, we were free!

When Rodrigo and Ciro left with Victor Polay, Pedro took over operational control of the escape. Armed with the walkie-talkie, he called Valentina, section chief of the MRTA women prisoners in the admissions building, and informed her that Team B was on the way. The group of six men, also clad in black and wearing tennis shoes, filed down the inner stairway and dropped through the manhole from which Pedro's Team A had emerged only a few minutes earlier. Here, they took the sewage duct leading in the opposite direction from the one that Team A had followed, and they had only to pass beneath Pavilion 1-B, 1-A and the kitchen area before arriving at the door leading to the admissions building where the women were waiting on the second floor.

Pancho was the leader of Team B wich was responsible for freeing the women prisoners. He had been charged with responsibility Team B at the same time that Pedro took over Team A and was the only one of his group who had known about the tunnel before it was opened the previous evening. He was armed with a pistol and a submachinegun, and the others carried pistols and razor-sharp *chavetas*. They had covered the route in total darkness many times before while patiently applying caustic soda to the welded seams of the metal door that stood between them and the hospital infirmary on the ground floor of the building.

This time, they carried two metal bars and cloth pads with them. Pancho left one man as lookout at the entrance to Pavilions 1-A and 1-B, and when they arrived at the infirmary door, they pulled its loosened lower corner back and used the bars and pads to silently bend the metal sheet back on itself to form a triangular opening through which they could crawl.

There was dim light through the infirmary windows, enough to see by, and the five men padded noiselessly down the corridor, inspecting the doctor's office, the nurses' area, the sickbay, and the padlocked medical supplies cubicle. Ordinarily, there were two nurses on duty each night, but since this was Sunday they found the area empty except for one newly-arrived prisoner who had not yet been assigned quarters in a pavilion. They awoke him silently, bound and gagged him and left one of the team standing over him with a *chaveta* at his throat.

Pancho and his second made their way to the end of the hall, where a barred door stood between them and access to the women's section.

None of the nine MRTA women prisoners had known of the existence of the tunnel until Pablo came to deliver the walkie-talkie and pick up Victor Polay's dinner the previous evening. Some weeks previously, however, Valentina had been informed that a team from 2-A was opening an underground route to the admissions building to bring the MRTA woman to Pavilion 2-A in the event of a prison riot such as the one which had led to the *Sendero* massacre a few years earlier. She was told to prepare an alternative route to lead her group to 2-A in case the first plan had to be canceled.

Besides the nine members of the MRTA in admissions, there were two "independent" political prisoners who were not affiliated with either the MRTA or the *Sendero Luminoso*. They were on good terms with the MRTA girls, but one of them, Valentina decided, was a bit too friendly with the female prison guards, so both had to be neutralized. One of the MRTA women had given birth the previous month. The baby had been turned over to her parents, but the new mother was suffering from a uterine infection and had not fully recovered. Another of the nine had a kidney infection and a third had a back injury as a consequence of her "interrogation" by DIRCOTE.

In her first radio communication with Rodrigo, Valentina outlined the problem of the three *compañeras* who would probably need help and guaranteed that she would deal with the two "independents." She surreptitiously passed the news to the rest of the group that the escape would take place early the following morning, and before dinner was served saw to it that liberal doses of crushed sleeping pills were stirred into the food of the two independents. Despite their efforts to display a calm façade, the girls found it impossible to conceal the electric tension that gripped all of them. One of the independents ate her dinner docilely and half an hour later yawned and retired to her bunk. The other, a sharp-eyed intuitive, only picked at her food and, after washing her utensils, settled down before the TV set and observed the comings and goings to Valentina's cell.

Valentina organized her troops into three groups. The three most athletic girls formed a rearguard unit armed with bottles—their only weapons; their task was to deal with any Republicans who tried to enter the area through the door leading to the front balcony while the escape was under way. The second group, composed of the three ailing *compañeras*, was to stand watch over the two independents, while Valentina and the remaining two dealt with the barred gate that separated their quarters from the stairway leading down to the infirmary.

This gate was the only remaining obstacle to the escape route leading through the underground ducts. The girls had been unable to obtain or make a duplicate key, but the previous week Margarita had boldly smuggled a hydraulic automobile jack into Canto Grande, concealed under a five-pound slab of brisket. When she received word that Team B was making its way to admissions, Valentina and her team were to insert the powerful instrument between two of the vertical bars in the gate and jack them apart sufficiently that the girls could slip through the opening.

We had the lights off in the corridor so we could move freely, and we kept the television going at a low volume Valentina told us. Finally, the second independent said goodnight and went off to bed. We left the rear guard watching TV and dispersed normally to our own cells — not to sleep, but to lie awake waiting for the operation to start.

At 3 a.m. we woke the two independents quietly, explained that we were breaking out of prison and had to leave them behind, bound and gagged, so the prison authorities couldn't accuse them of being accomplices.

They cooperated cheerfully, wished us good luck, and we even postponed tying them up and gagging them until the last minute so they wouldn't suffer unnecessarily. We had posted lookouts at both the inside and outside windows from the beginning, and there had been no unusual movements from the guard barracks or inside the central patio. We observed the changing of the guard at 3:00 and we saw *Comandante* Polay appear at his window a little after 3:45 a signal that he was going out over the roof.

We said goodbye to the independents then and took our positions in the corridor. My team had the jack, and we calculated it would take ten to fifteen minutes to pry the bars apart. The other two girls were about to set up the jack when we heard a noise from the infirmary and saw figures coming toward us. We ducked out of sight until we identified them as Pancho and two other *compañeros*. Pancho passed me a pistol and told me the infirmary was empty except for one common prisoner whom they had bound and gagged. The other two men were setting up the jack between the bars when someone made a false move and the jack handle fell to the floor with a clang. We all went to super-alert and heard a prison guard climbing up the front stairway to investigate the sound. He unlocked the balcony door, entered, and as he stepped into the corridor one of the rearguard girls bopped him over the head with her bottle. He let out a yelp and went down. He scrambled up again and went running down the stairs with all of us behind him. He was really one scared Republican. In the cubicle at the foot of the stairway was another male guard and a female guard. I waved my pistol at them as I went past, and none of them made a move to stop us or to sound an alarm. All nine of us streaked through the admissions corridor and made for the chainlink fence in front of Pavilion 2-A. It was about two-and-a-half meters high, and the toes of our slippers didn't fit into the diagonal squares, but we pushed the three sick girls up so they could grip the tube along the top and pull themselves up and over, and the rest of us were so full of adrenalin that we can't remember how we made it. There were several *compas* armed with combat rifles waiting inside the fence, and one of them pushed us through the small door leading into no-man's-land and we started going down the hole one after another. I started crawling, because the tunnel was small, but one of the diggers waiting at the bottom told me: "On your feet, *compañera*," and I discovered I could walk in a crouch. He asked me who the sick girls were, and I told him which two particularly needed help. He said there were mine cars to carry them out and left me. I went creeping along, doubled over, and when there was more room overhead I started running, because I knew the guards had been alerted and they'd soon be after us. There were lights at intervals, but despite that I banged my head on a protruding rock so hard it knocked me down, and after that I was more careful.

Pancho watched the girls hastening out the balcony door, then turned to his comrades.

"They're using the alternate plan," he said. "Let's get out of here."

Team B turned back and retraced its steps with Pancho in the lead.

It was pitch dark, and we couldn't hurry because it was slippery underfoot. We couldn't so much as touch the walls to guide ourselves. Besides being slimy, there were bare electric wires running along them. We got back to the entrance to 2-A, replaced the manhole cover and climbed up the interior stairway to the fourth floor. There wasn't a soul there, so we made our way down the outside stairway to the ground floor. I dropped behind, looking for Pedro to report what had happened, but he was nowhere to be seen. When I got to the mess hall I didn't know what to do because the escape window was closed, and I didn't know which one it was.

The common prisoners were already milling around in our downstairs quarters, dividing up the belongings we had left behind, and Pedro wasn't there either. At that point one of the independent prisoner came up to and said, "It's over here, *compañero,*" and he led me to the right window. The last man out had kicked the box away that propped the window open, but now the independent climbed up on a bench alongside me and held the window open while I slid out.

One of Ernesto's rearguard was waiting at the hole and slid into it as he saw me coming. I followed him, and there was some confusion at the bottom. Jaime and Pedro were down there, making a head-count of the people as they came through.

"We have to wait for the last man," he said. "There's still one missing."

"No, no, no," I told him. "I'm the last man; let's get out of here."

We started stumbling along in the pitch dark, because one of the women had snagged her foot in the electric wiring system and pulled out the plug.

The sudden blackout in the latter portion of the tunnel disconcerted the women and Ernesto's rearguard team. The tunnel transformed into a confusion of bodies, crawling or groping their way along the walls in total darkness. Jaime was behind the final group and the only one with a flashlight.

They all came to a stop because there was an obstruction ahead — Jaime recalled — and I had to squeeze past all of them, telling them to keep calm, until I got to the bottleneck. It was caused by the *compañera* who had just had a baby. She was being pushed along in the mine car by one of the other diggers, and in the darkness he couldn't control the direction. We got her out of the car and pushed it into a niche so the others could pass. The girl was exhausted and on the point of collapse, and I had to coax her, urge her to summon all her strength, and pull her along by the hands. The lights in the *La Lucha Continúa* section were functioning, but I had to half-push, half-carry her to the very end. I helped her up the vertical ladder and into the safe house. I left her with others and went to look for a pair of pants and a shirt, because I was smeared with mud and wearing only a pair of briefs. By the time I got dressed, the last of the women and the rear guard were climbing out of the tunnel and getting into the old pickup truck, and I joined them.

Luis Angel was delivering a load of escapees to the temporary safe house Armando had arranged earlier, and the driver of the old pickup was not familiar with the Canto

Grande area. At a crucial intersection, he took the wrong turning and started heading back toward the penitentiary. Antonio, who was in the cab, seized him by the arm before they ran into a guard checkpoint, "This is the wrong way," he hissed. "Turn around."

The driver overrode the curbing as he wrenched the wheel, and there was a clang and a scraping sound as the overloaded truck lurched off in the opposite direction. They reached the correct highway and picked up speed until the smoking fumes of overheated oil billowed up under the hood and drifted into the cab and rear of the truck. A hundred meters further on, the motor seized up and died. During the abrupt turnaround a hidden obstacle had ruptured the radiator; the starter motor whined, but the truck refused to budge.

Antonio seized an empty oil container from beneath the driver's seat and ran down the road in search of water. The third house down had an outdoor faucet, and he filled the container quietly, returned, and splashed the contents over the smoking block. Two more trips restored a minimal water level in the leaking radiator. At Antonio's urging, five *compas* leaped out of the back of the truck and helped him push while the driver expended the remaining battery charge to turn over the starter motor. At the last moment the motor caught, the exhaust belched smoke and the helpers clambered aboard as the truck ground into first gear and picked up speed down the highway.

The first glimmers of dawn dispelled the blackness over the Andes as the truck spluttered and roared toward its destination. In the truck bed, the last fugitives from Canto Grande gripped their weapons with bloodless knuckles and peered out the back for signs of pursuit.

Pichirulo, the only non-MRTA militant in the vehicle, was over-stimulated. Wedged between Valentina and a member of Ernesto's rearguard team, he kept up a running commentary about their possible whereabouts until the latter asked him to kindly keep quiet. The truck swung left at an intersection, and in the cab Antonio told the driver:

"Pull over. We're getting close."

The truck stopped alongside the curbing, its motor running, and Antonio climbed down from the cab, went to the back and beckoned to Pichirulo.

"This is as far as you go," he grinned, handing him a thin wad of bills, "and this will help you get started. Thanks for everything."

Pichirulo pocketed the money and peered up expectantly at Antonio, who jerked a thumb back toward the intersection. After a moment's hesitation, he started walking, advanced some thirty meters and looked back over his shoulder without stopping. The truck remained at the curbing, panting heavily, and Antonio stood there, motionless. Pirichulo broke into a trot, heading for the bus stop on the main thoroughfare. He doubled his distance from the truck, stopped again breathing heavily, and turned around. The truck was still there, its motor idling and Antonio was still watching him, motionless. Pichirulo raised both arms and waggled his hands at the escapees, a grin splitting his features. The *compas* in the back of the getaway vehicle leaned out and waved back at him, and so did Antonio.

Pichirulo turned again and, head down, chuckling to himself, broke into a run toward his new life. It had been a clean breakout, one for the Guinness records, and he'd been a part of it. They couldn't take that away from him.

EPILOGUE

In various safe houses scattered through Lima, the jubilant escapees listened to news broadcasts the morning of July 9, giving the first accounts of their feat.

In one of those safe houses, some six weeks later, we started interviewing the protagonists of this story. Margarita and Paloma were the safe-house keepers, and one section of the house was devoted to a week-long politico-military school for twenty-five of the Canto Grande escapees who were being assigned to guerrilla columns in the mountains.

After rendezvousing in a central café and exchanging recognition signals, Paloma and René, who was Paloma's current safe house "husband," drove us through the streets of Lima and along one trafficless street, ordering us to squeeze down in the back seat of the sedan while Paloma pulled a plastic sheet over our heads. We drove for another twenty minutes before René turned, braked to a stop, and got out to open a garage door. He drove in and locked the door behind him. Paloma handed each of us a hood with "MRTA" lettered in red on the forehead and two eyeholes.

"Put them on," she told us, and then corrected Claribel. "No, the eyeholes go in back."

She and René ushered us out of the car, totally blindfolded by the hoods, and we were led by the hand into the safe house. We were walked through various rooms and finally up a flight of stairs into the bedroom that was to serve as our confinement cell for the following week. By the second day of interviews, we were adjudged reliable and were permitted to come downstairs, unhooded, and take our meals with Paloma, Margarita, and René after the "students" had been served. Margarita, her eyes shining, told us how, several days before our arrival, they had received another consignment of Canto Grande escapees and she had led one of the hooded boys upstairs to the schoolroom.

"I recognized his hands," she said triumphantly, "it was Roberto. And I squeezed his hands and whispered 'Roberto.'"

During our week-long stay we taped some fifty-five hours of interviews with twenty of the people who had planned and dug the tunnel or had organized the escape from inside Canto Grande. Victor Polay donated eight hours of his time and after he had given us a detailed résumé of the project plan and an account of his own experience as a prisoner in the *venusterio*, we started talking about the MRTA organization and the role it was playing in the present historic juncture in Peru.

During our short stay in Lima prior to being ushered into the safe house, and from the background reading we had done, we had formed a vision of the MRTA as occupying an uncomfortably cramped political space between the fanatical Maoist visionaries of *Sendero Luminoso* (Shining Path) on the extreme left and the *Izquierda Unida* (United Left) which constituted the leftist parliamentary opposition to the governing APRA party. The *Senderistas* and the MRTA were the only two guerrilla groups in Peru that had taken up arms against the government. This situation led to our first political question:

Many years ago, both Fidel Castro and Che Guevara warned that as long as an electoral alternative existed in any country, a guerrilla movement was doomed to failure. Today, we have "death squad" democracies in Guatemala and El Salvador, a limited democracy under the thumb of Pinochet in Chile, and IMF democracies in Brazil, Argentina and Mexico, to cite a few diverse examples. Do the warnings of Fidel and Che still hold true in this new situation?

VICTOR POLAY: Latin America has changed in the thirty years since the Cuban liberation struggle. We have had the "gorilla" dictatorships in Chile, Uruguay, and Argentina, with their sequels of disappearances and assassinations. Today, these have apparently been replaced by democratic governments, but the "dirty war" is their fundamental component.

In the case of Peru, Fernando Belaúnde, who became president in 1980, had the dubious privilege of inaugurating parliamentary democracies in the continent that at the same time developed counter-insurgency warfare as a principal means of dominating popular movements. According to human rights organizations, this political violence has claimed more than 20,000 victims since then, more than 3,000 of whom have disappeared, and these levels have increased steadily under the government of Alan García.

In Peru, there exists not only political violence but a structural violence that makes it impossible for the average Peruvian to develop as a human being should. He is confronted day by day with economic violence, social violence, and racial violence as well. The right to work doesn't exist for the great majority of the population.

President Fujimori himself recognizes that only fifteen percent of the population receives wages that permit them to maintain an adequate standard of living. Seventy-five percent of the population is under-employed, earning less than the minimum wage — which is the equivalent of a paltry fifteen dollars per month. And the remaining ten percent have no income whatsoever.

What I am saying is that a structural violence exists that denies the Peruvian people the right to a job, the right to a roof over their heads, the right to health care, the right to an education, and even the very right to eat. This social violence is reflected in the fact that more than 100 of every 1,000 children born die shortly after birth. Add to that 5,000 children between the ages of one and five who die each year of malnutrition or curable diseases. Over the past ten years some 50,000 children have died this way. You can see that this ingrown social violence, only taking into account the situation of children under five, has caused two and a half times more deaths than the political violence over the same period.

In addition to the above, there exists an endemic racial violence in Peru. Ever since the Republic was founded, the white race — first the offspring of Spaniards and later the sons of European immigrants — has controlled the power and wealth of the nation. They look down on the great majority of the population: the indigenous peoples, the mestizos, the blacks, and the Asians.

We of the MRTA cannot accept that democracy is reduced to holding elections once every five years, which means the people extend a blank check to leaders who can do as they please for the next five years. Alan García promised he would carry out a revolution that was nationalistic, democratic, and popular, and we are all witnesses to the practical consequences of that remote revolution.

Instead, we postulate a higher form of democracy: we're speaking of a people's democracy, a democracy in which popular traditions and mass organizations can exercise direct control of the instruments and the policies of state power, which must respond to popular needs and aspirations. And we believe that all forms of struggle — revolutionary struggle and popular resistance, armed struggle and peaceful struggle — are necessary to transform the structure of this society. We don't want cosmetic changes, merely to change things a little bit so that nothing changes. We want substantial changes, so that Peru, which is suffering from centuries of accumulated frustrations, undergoes a radical transformation that strikes at the roots of the existing system.

It is our conviction that great evils require great solutions, and the only road the Peruvian people can travel for the sake of sheer survival, for self-realization as human beings, for seizing control of their own destinies and realizing their hopes and dreams, is the path of a revolutionary process.

We have always made clear that the MRTA is an instrument of struggle of the Peruvian people, and not an end in itself. We recognize the fact that there are other struggles and other organizations that must contribute to the liberation of our country, and for that reason the future must be built on the base of multi-party democracy, and we welcome the participation of all the leftist forces, including the bases of APRA and the democratic and patriotic sectors of the armed forces and the police.

Given the general dissolution of the socialist bloc in Eastern Europe, and with Vargas Llosa predicting the end of communism, what objective basis does the MRTA have for insisting on a socialist solution in Peru?

What we want to make clear is that the *Movimiento Revolucionario Tupac Amaru* is the most genuine expression of national reality, of Latin American reality. The MRTA was not born with the support of, or in the shadow of, the international communist movement, be it pro-China, pro-Soviet, Albanian, Yugoslav, or whatever adjective you wish to use. It is true that there are profound changes underway in the former socialist bloc, but these are a product of their own reality. We don't feel that their failures to construct a workable socialism need affect our organization.

The MRTA never proclaimed itself to be communist nor to be the repository of "real socialism." From the outset we have been jealous of preserving our political and ideological autonomy, and we are profoundly *Mariáteguistas* in the sense that the Peruvian revolution cannot be a carbon copy or clone of any other but must respond to the Peruvian situation.

And what is the Peruvian situation?

It is the fact that dependent capitalism, the form in which the ruling class has exercised its domination over the people, the form in which it has organized the state and society, has been a dismal failure. Capitalism has never solved any vital problem in Peru. We can say, clearly and plainly, that in the Andean countries of Latin America, and particularly in Peru, dependent capitalism — capitalism subordinated to North American imperialism — has been a total disaster. It has not solved the problems of hunger, jobs, health, education, or housing. That form of social organization has to be overturned by a revolution that has as its goals the collective well-being of society and the humanization of each individual and that places these goals above private profit, personal advantage, and the profit margin of an individual company.

If such a change were to take place, how could a socialist Peru insert itself into a world economy based on free enterprise? Autarchy is hardly possible these days, so how could Peru use its resources to elevate the general standard of living?

We believe that socialism in Peru is the answer to a real need, and it will be reached by following a uniquely Peruvian path. We also believe that we are not the only ones who are searching for a socialistic solution. In Asia, Africa, and in Europe itself, not to mention the rest of Latin America, peoples are exploring new paths, in accordance with their own characteristics and particular needs, to resolve problems of injustice, and lack of freedom and national sovereignty in the face of imperialist domination. Obviously, we should make common cause with these peoples whose objectives are similar to our own.

In addition, Peru is on a par with the other Andean countries, such as Bolivia, Ecuador, Colombia, and Chile, and we think that now, more than ever, we are on the point of realizing the dream of the Founding Fathers of independence: Bolivar, San Martín, and Martí. We possess a continental patrimony, and the hour has come to join together in regional blocs and eventually to construct a new fatherland on a continental scale. This is not a romantic dream, but a stern necessity. We are witnessing a rapid integration of Europe; the United States wants to integrate Latin America in a common market under its hegemony. If we want to create an important presence in the international community of nations, Latin America must unify its economies and integrate its productive apparatus, its political and social systems, in order to enter the twenty-first century on equal terms with other regional blocs.

How does the MRTA view the *Sendero Luminoso*? Do you see it as a competitor for the position of revolutionary vanguard of the Peruvian people?

As I said previously, the MRTA was created to contribute to the transformation of Peruvian society, and we do not measure our objectives in terms of competition with the *Senderistas* or with any other leftist party or group.

In its origins, the *Sendero Luminoso* set out to channel the rebellious sentiments of certain segments of the population, but its political tactics and military actions have developed in such away as to set it against the Peruvian people and the popular organizations. The *Senderistas* have a very sectarian, very dogmatic view of the revolutionary process in Peru. They believe they are the only revolutionary organization in Peru — or in the world, for that matter. This has led them to develop a series of terroristic methods that we feel are totally counterproductive.

We consider them to be profoundly mistaken in attempting to impose their own forms of organization on the natural organizations of the Peruvian people, and we believe that no revolutionary struggle can be aimed against the masses of the people. When they attack labor unions and peasant communities and assassinate popular leaders, they are distancing themselves from the people. They are isolating themselves politically by the use of such tactics, and we believe that, fundamentally, their defeat must take place on the political battlefield rather than through military repression. The *Senderistas* don't bother to explain their tactics or goals, whereas we of the MRTA take care to publicly explain and justify every action we carry out. Our political platform is fundamental, and therefore military actions must be subordinate to political considerations in every situation.

It appears to us that the *Sendero Luminoso* is, objectively, a counterrevolutionary phenomenon in that their repugnant terrorist tactics virtually justify in the eyes of the people the increasing repression on the part of the police and the armed forces. Could you comment on this?

Yes. We have here a curious phenomenon that has occurred more than once before in history: the political extremes meet and use each other. The most reactionary sectors of the dominant class and the armed forces, of course, seek a

Pinochet-type solution for Peru, and they are the ones who inflate the *Senderista* phenomenon in the public media. Their purpose is to justify increased levels of repression and to provoke a fascist coup. On the other hand, the *Senderistas* with their provocative terrorist actions are working toward that same goal. The two extremes need each other in the same way that policemen and jailers need bandits and robbers to justify their existence.

Our interview with Victor Polay continued, but lack of space prevents its total reproduction here. As this manuscript was being finalized in April 1992, however, Polay's prescience in his final statement here was borne out on the Peruvian national stage as President Fujimori dissolved Parliament, suspended the judiciary system, and carried out a self-inflicted coup d'état that effectively turned over the keys of power to the Peruvian armed forces.

CURBSTONE PRESS, INC.

is a non-profit publishing house dedicated to literature that reflects a commitment to social change, with an emphasis on contemporary writing from Latin America and Latino communities in the United States. Curbstone presents writers who give voice to the unheard in a language that goes beyond denunciation to celebrate, honor and teach. Curbstone builds bridges between its writers and the public – from inner-city to rural areas, colleges to community centers, children to adults. Curbstone seeks out the highest aesthetic expression of the dedication to human rights and intercultural understanding: poetry, fiction, testimonies, photography.

This mission requires more than just producing books. It requires ensuring that as many people as possible know about these books and read them. To achieve this, a large portion of Curbstone's schedule is dedicated to arranging tours and programs for its authors, working with public school and university teachers to enrich curricula, reaching out to underserved audiences by donating books and conducting readings and community programs, and promoting discussion in the media. It is only through these combined efforts that literature can truly make a difference.

Curbstone Press, like all non-profit presses, depends on the support of individuals, foundations, and government agencies to bring you, the reader, works of literary merit and social significance which might not find a place in profit-driven publishing channels. Our sincere thanks to the many individuals who support this endeavor and to the following foundations and government agencies: ADCO Foundation, Witter Bynner Foundation for Poetry, Inc., Connecticut Commission on the Arts, Connecticut Arts Endowment Fund, Ford Foundation, Lannan Foundation, LEF Foundation, Lila Wallace-Reader's Digest Fund, The Andrew W. Mellon Foundation, National Endowment for the Arts, and The Plumsock Fund.

Please support Curbstone's efforts to present the diverse voices and views that make our culture richer. Tax-deductible donations can be made to Curbstone Press, 321 Jackson Street, Willimantic, CT 06226.
phone: (203) 423-5110   e-mail: curbston@connix.com
visit our WWW site at http://www.connix.com/~curbston/